D0466101

CARAVAGGIO

CARAVAGGIO

A PASSIONATE LIFE

DESMOND SEWARD

WILLIAM MORROW AND COMPANY, INC. NEW YORK

Portrait of Caravaggio by Ottavio Leoni. Although Leoni did not draw from life, this is the best contemporary likeness, other than the self-portraits.

It is the policy of William Morrow and Company, Inc., and its imprints and affiliates, recognizing the importance of preserving what has been written, to print the books we publish on acid-free paper, and we exert our best efforts to that end.

Seward, Desmond, 1935–
Caravaggio : a passionate life / Desmond Seward. — 1st ed.
p. cm.
Includes bibliographical references and index.
ISBN 0-688-15032-2 (alk. paper)
1. Caravaggio, Michelangelo Merisi da, 1573–1610. 2. Painters — Italy—Biography. I. Title.
ND623.C26S48 1998
759.5—dc21
[b] 98-38694
CIP

Printed in the United States of America

First Edition

1 2 3 4 5 6 7 8 9 10

BOOK DESIGN BY LEAH LOCOCO

www.williammorrow.com.

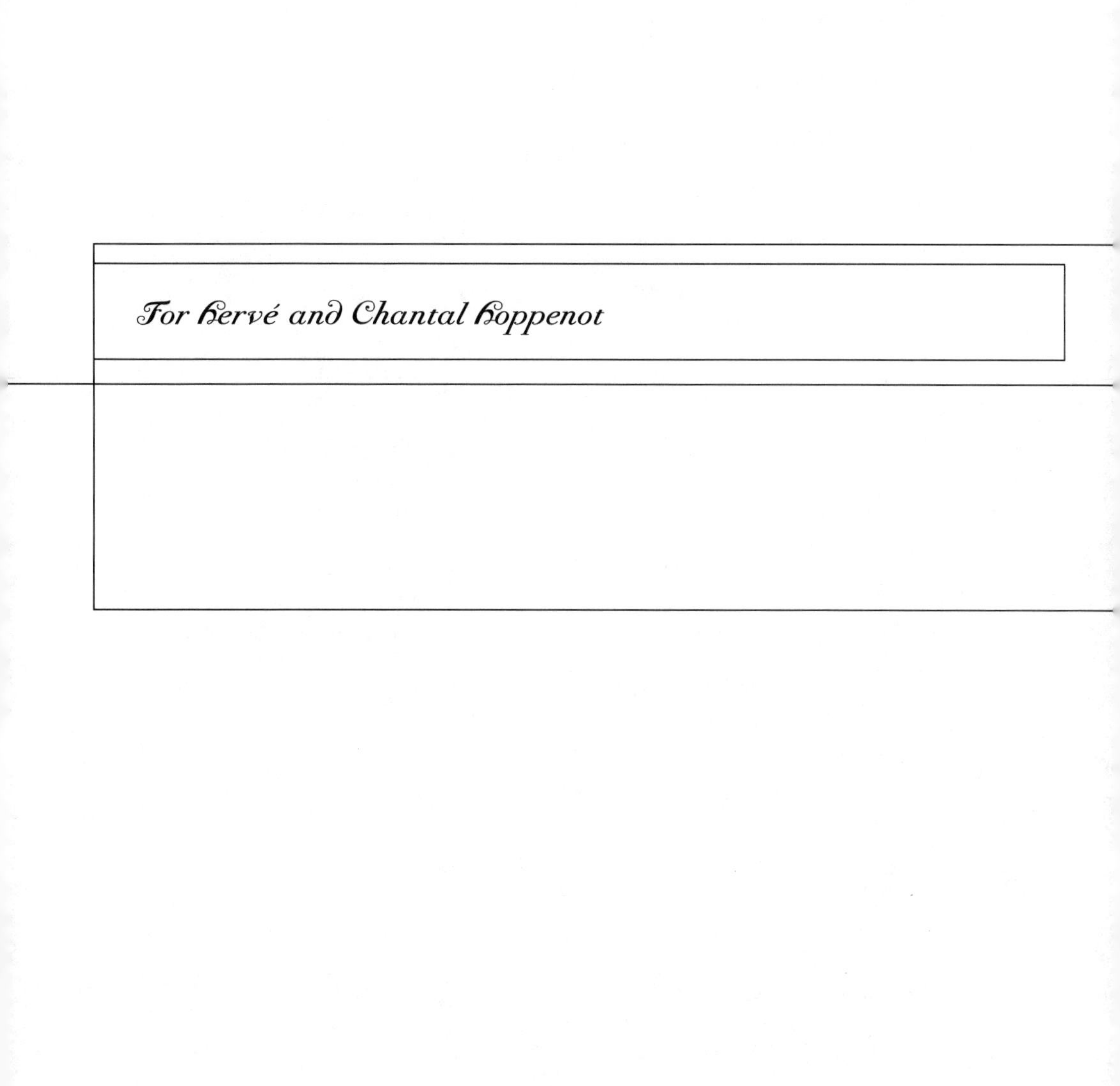

For Hervé and Chantal Hoppenot

PREFACE

On a hot July afternoon in 1610, while the enervating sirocco blew and most sensible people were in bed behind closed shutters, an unkempt little man was boarding a felucca from the beach below a great lady's palace on the Chiaia at Naples. Thin and sickly, he was in his late thirties. Coarse features and uneasy brown eyes glared from a sallow face, even uglier than usual because of barely healed sword cuts, fringed by long, uncombed hair and a short, untrimmed beard. His black clothes were the latest Spanish fashion, but they looked as if he had slept in them, while on a gold chain around his neck he wore the enameled cross of a Knight of Malta. He seemed to be in constant pain. Every now and then his scowl turned into a sneer as he burst out with some jibe at the sailors.

Anyone watching must have wondered why he was not embarking on one of his order's galleys, the fastest ships in the Mediterranean. A tiny felucca was the cheapest form of transport available, with two stumpy masts and four oars, without an awning for shelter from sun, wind, or rain.

He cursed the crew as they took his scanty baggage on board. They did what he wanted, not because of his threats but because he obviously had plenty of money and was paying for his passage in gold. The teenaged boy carrying his sword in its velvet scabbard handed it to him over the gunwale. With a three-foot blade, a rapier was too long for such a short man to wear at his side, though he plainly knew how to use it. He also wore a large dagger, which he never took off, not even in bed.

While his bags were being stowed, together with some odd rolls of canvas, he kept glancing up nervously, scanning the deserted beach. Here clearly was someone who felt that pursuing enemies were closing in.

His felucca was bound for Rome, though en route she would put in at obscure havens. Whatever the weather, she would hug the coast, her crew camping ashore each night. They dared not put out into the open sea for fear of pirates. A distant white sail on the horizon could all too easily be a Barbary corsair, meaning death or slavery.

For years, the passenger had been on the run, after killing a man in a duel. A few months before, he had been imprisoned, in a dungeon called the "Birdcage," for half killing another man, and only recently the latter's hired assassins had barely failed to murder him. They were still hoping for a second chance, lurking outside the old lady's palace on the Chiaia, where he had been hiding.

Despite the dangers and discomforts of the voyage ahead, he was feverishly impatient to set sail, and not merely because of his enemies. He wanted to reach Rome as fast as possible, since he had every reason to think that great things awaited him there. He did not know that he would be dead within little more than a week. He called himself "Fra' Michelangelo da Caravaggio."

Born in 1571, Caravaggio is one of the best known of all the great painters. Each year his pictures find new admirers from among an amazingly wide cross section of humanity. Many lavishly illustrated books on him have been published, and his paintings have become increasingly familiar, in particular *The Lute Player, Rest on the Flight into Egypt, Judith and Holofernes, The Supper at Emmaus,* and *The Beheading of St. John.*

This is a book about Caravaggio the man, rather than Caravaggio the painter. Although man and painter are inseparable, too many studies by art historians have left important questions about him unanswered. They do not investigate his world and how it shaped him; nor do they stress sufficiently the inner conflict he suffered, or the sheer drama of his life. He soared from obscurity to international acclaim, and then, after his fatal duel, became an outlaw who eventually died friendless on a beach in the ironical knowledge that he was about to receive a full pardon. This biography is meant for the general reader, not the specialist. It does not attempt to analyze his paintings, nor to question attributions. It uses his pictures to peer into his mind.

Some years ago, an extremely successful film, *Amadeus,* contrasted Mozart's music with his dingy private life. There could be no greater contrast than that between Caravaggio's painting and *his* private life. On canvas he was a spiritual genius whose profound religious statements touch the hearts of unbelievers as well as believers. Yet, in Bernard Berenson's words, he was "quick-tempered and bad-tempered, intolerant, devious, jealous, spiteful, quarrelsome, a street-brawler, a homicide, and perhaps a homosexual. He was endowed with innumerable gifts, but with none for decent living." Even during his lifetime, Caravaggio's long-suffering protector, Cardinal del Monte, credited him with "a wildly capricious brain." Another patron thought that his brain was "twisted." More than one prince of the Church was ready to overlook his sins for the sake of his genius, but they could not save him from himself.

To some extent, his violent streak can be attributed to the Italy into which he was born at the end of the Renaissance. It was a country that shocked foreigners, inspiring such plays as *The White Devil* and *The Duchess of Malfi.* Some historians argue that Jacobean England's view of Italy was distorted by Protestant prejudice, but it was not so far from the truth; murders as terrible as anything in Webster's tragedies took place. Although it was illegal to carry arms without a license, most Italian gentlemen wore a rapier and a dagger, partly for protection against the robbers swarming in the streets but also for fighting duels. Caravaggio fought in at least two duels, probably more. What makes this so puzzling is his obvious sensitivity and compassion.

If he was one of the most wonderful painters who have ever lived, he was also one of the most mysterious. Did he really visit Venice when he was a young man? Was he forced to leave his native city of Milan, and never return, because of a murder? Was he a homosexual? And who was the enemy who waged a relentless vendetta against him?

One of the reasons Caravaggio is so fascinating is that he put so much of his troubled personality into his paintings. In pictures he produced during times of great stress, one can often detect his wretchedness and exhaustion. What we know of his short existence was filled with tragedy. His childhood in Milan was darkened by the bubonic plague that killed his father, his early manhood in Rome by poverty and discouragement. His few years of prosperity and fame were ruined by an uncontrollable temper, ending in his banishment as a murderer. And the pattern was to be repeated. Many of his last days were spent in fear and foreboding.

Modern research has added enormously to our information, yet we can often only say what we don't know about Caravaggio. No one familiar with his story can deny that his behavior was so full of contradictions that it sometimes defies analysis. Few if any really great artists have had a police record like his. He was obsessed with beheading, and he painted at least a dozen severed heads, including his own. I have done my modest best to understand what went on inside it.

ACKNOWLEDGMENTS

While writing this book I always kept in mind Alessandro Manzoni's helpful comment in *The Betrothed* on an obscure seventeenth-century official's behavior during the riots of Milan: "What else he did, we cannot tell, as he was quite alone and history can only guess. Luckily, it is quite used to doing so." If, in the absence of firm evidence, speculation about Caravaggio is sometimes inescapable, I have at least tried to avoid invention.

Among the many people who have helped me with advice or encouragement, I would particularly like to thank Canon John Azzopardi, Curator of the Cathedral Museum, Medina; Carol Bado; Professor Mario Bouhagiar of the University of Malta; Professor A. S. Ciechanowiecki; Anne Freedgood, my editor in New York, without whom this book would never have been written; Anna Somers-Cocks; Susan Mountgarret; and Fr. Marius Zerafa, Director of Museums, Valletta. I am also grateful to Sir Stephen and Lady Egerton for their hospitality in Rome in 1992, which enabled me to visit the exhibition *Caravaggio: Come nascono i Capolavori,* at the Palazzo Ruspoli; and to Peter and Margaret McCann for lending me their farmhouse on Gozo as a base for research on Malta.

Among others who have helped me, with much patience and kindness, are the staffs of the British Library, the National Fine Arts Library (London), the London Library, the Library of the National Gallery (London), and the National Library of Malta.

CONTENTS

PREFACE VII

ACKNOWLEDGMENTS XI

ILLUSTRATIONS XV

I: *Milan, 1571* 1

II: *Carlo Borromeo and the Plague, 1576-1578* 6

III: *Apprenticeship, 1584-1588* 9

IV: *The Counter-Reformation* 13

V: *The Flight from Milan, 1592* 17

VI: *Rome, 1592* 20

VII: *The Rulers of Rome, 1592* 25

VIII: *The Hack Painter, 1592-1596* 29

IX: *Cardinal del Monte, 1596* 34

X: *Palazzo Madama, 1596-1600* 38

XI: *Homosexual or Heterosexual? 1596-1600* 42

XII: *"Nature the only subject fit for his brush," 1596* 47

XIII: *The Year of Murders, 1599* 54

XIV: *The First Severed Heads, 1599* 59

XV: *The Contarelli Chapel, 1599–1600* 63

XVI: *The New Patrons, 1600-1602* 68

XVII: *The Swordsman, 1600-1606* 76

XVIII: *"Wonderful Things at Rome," 1603* 85

XIX: *The First Baroque Pope, 1605* 90

XX: *The Killing of Ranuccio Tommasoni, May 1606* 96

XXI: *Outlaw in the Roman Hills, Summer 1606* 101

XXII: *Interlude at Naples, 1606-1607* 106

XXIII: *The Neapolitan Altarpieces* 110

XXIV: *The Prior of Naples* 115

XXV: *The Knights of Malta, July 1607* 118

XXVI: *The Novice, 1607-1608* 122

XXVII: *The Grand Master* 127

XXVIII: *"Fra' Michelangelo," July 1608* 131

XXIX: *The Unknown Knight, September 1608* 135

XXX: *A Dungeon Called the "Birdcage," September 1608* 139

XXXI: *Syracuse, 1608-1609* 143

XXXII: *Messina, 1609* 149

XXXIII: *Palermo, 1609* 156

XXXIV: *"The Neapolitan Shrug," 1609* 159

XXXV: *"Puerto Hercules," July 1610* 166

EPILOGUE 171

APPENDIX: WHERE TO SEE CARAVAGGIO'S PICTURES 175

SOURCES 179

INDEX 193

Text photographs: Ottavio Leoni, *Portrait of Caravaggio*, page ii; Caravaggio: *Basket of Fruit*, page xii; *David with the Head of Goliath*, page xvi; *Conversion of St. Paul*, page xviii.

Illustrations following page 108:

Youth with a Basket of Fruit SCALA/ART RESOURCE, N.Y.

St. Francis in Ecstasy NIMATALLAH/ART RESOURCE, N.Y.

St. Catherine

Rest on the Flight into Egypt SCALA/ART RESOURCE, N.Y.

Judith and Holofernes NIMATALLAH/ART RESOURCE, N.Y.

Martyrdom of St. Matthew ALINARI/ART RESOURCE, N.Y.

Basket of Fruit SCALA/ART RESOURCE, N.Y.

Conversion of St. Paul SCALA/ART RESOURCE, N.Y.

The Madonna di Loreto SCALA/ART RESOURCE, N.Y.

Supper at Emmaus NIMATALLAH/ART RESOURCE, N.Y.

Portrait of a Knight of Malta

Alof de Wignancourt, Grand Master of the Order of Malta ERICH LESSING/ART RESOURCE, N.Y.

St. Jerome SCALA/ART RESOURCE, N.Y.

Beheading of St. John ERICH LESSING/ART RESOURCE, N.Y.

Raising of Lazarus

David with the Head of Goliath SCALA/ART RESOURCE, N.Y.

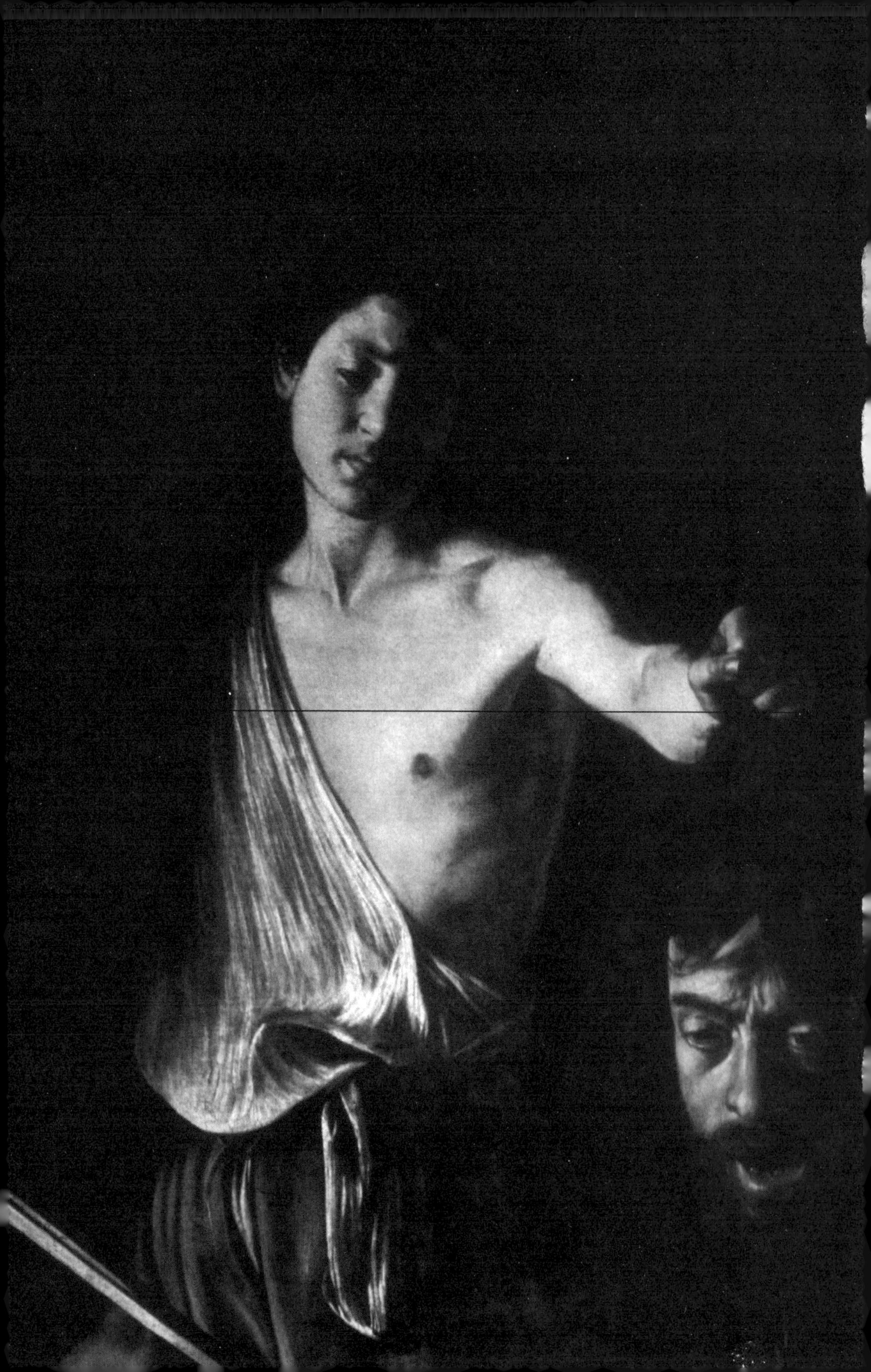

". . .like the hero of a modern play,

except that he happened to paint very well."

KENNETH CLARK, CIVILISATION

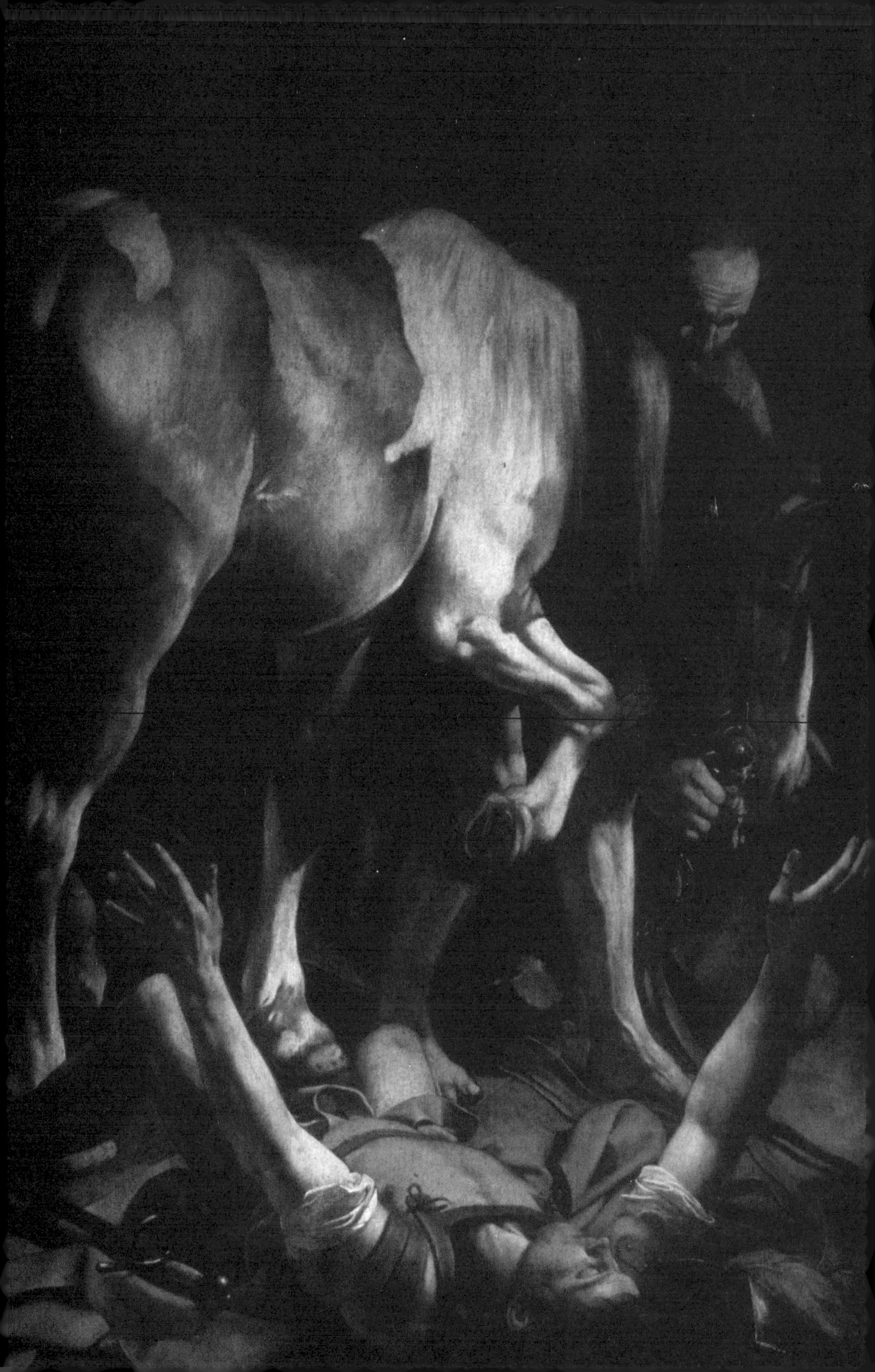

CARAVAGGIO

Milan, 1571

About 1596, shortly after Caravaggio went to live in Cardinal del Monte's household in Rome, his brother Giovan Battista, soon to become a friar, called on the cardinal and explained who he was, adding that Caravaggio might not wish to see him. It was clear that he loved his brother, so del Monte told him to come back in three days' time. Summoning Caravaggio, the cardinal asked if he had any relatives. He answered that he had none. Del Monte then questioned men from Caravaggio's part of Italy. They confirmed that he had a younger brother. When Giovan Battista returned, the cardinal sent for Caravaggio, who insisted that Giovan Battista was not his brother.

"I've come from very far away to see you, and, having seen you, I've done what I set out to do," Giovan Battista told him. "I've no need for you to help me or help my children, because I won't have any. As for your own children, if God answers my prayers to see you married with a family, I hope he blesses you in them, as I shall ask his Divine Majesty at my Masses, and as your sister will in her prayers." But Caravaggio refused even to say good-bye.

This story comes from *Considerations on Painting* by Giulio Mancini

(1558–1630), a dilettante physician from Sienna who, although he never met Caravaggio, knew at least one of his sitters. He tells the story as an example of Caravaggio's oddity. Yet Caravaggio's refusal to acknowledge Giovan Battista may have been due to doubts about his paternity. The marriage of his father's employer, Francesco Sforza, Marchese di Caravaggio, to Princess Costanza Colonna had gone badly at first, and Caravaggio's parents could have spoken about their quarrels in front of him, although they were over by the time he was born. It is not entirely impossible that he imagined he was an illegitimate Sforza.

Fantasies apart, he was the son of Fermo di Bernardino Merisi of Caravaggio. Two early sources say Fermo was a mason, Bellori apparently copying Baglione. But Baglione was a bitter enemy of Caravaggio, against whom he once brought a libel action, and his account, written after Caravaggio was safely dead, is often malicious. Mancini, the most reliable of the early sources, informs us that Fermo was "master of the household and architect to the Marchese di Caravaggio," while documentary evidence shows that he was a small landowner on the fringe of the lesser gentry.

Fermo appears to have been on very friendly terms with the marchese, who was a witness at his wedding to Lucia Aratori on 14 January 1571, in the church of Santi Petri e Paolo at Caravaggio. No birth certificate has ever been found, but it is now generally agreed that he was born in either Caravaggio or Milan at the end of September, a few days before the great victory over the Turks at Lepanto. He may well have descended from a family of architects. A Giulio Merisi had been an architect in Rome, where he is said to have built the Palazzo Capodiferro Spada for Cardinal Capodiferro. Fermo, an architect himself, named his son after another architect. Ironically, in the Milanese dialect "Michelangelo" could easily be confused with "Michelaccio," a roving ne'er-do-well from Lombard folklore.

Just over forty kilometers east of Milan, the tiny town of Caravaggio was close to the Venetian border. Fermo owned a house at the Folceria Gate, with a little estate outside the walls. The town's only distinguished son was Pollidoro da Caravaggio, a pupil of Titian, murdered in 1543, who may have been a Knight of Malta.

The surrounding countryside, the plain of Lombardy, was very fertile, irrigated by innumerable canals. In 1608 the English tourist Tom Coryate, viewing it from the roof of the Duomo at Milan, called the plain "the garden of Italy," marveling at its orchards, vineyards, and pastures. When Henry James undertook the same interminable climb to the Duomo's roof in 1872, it looked very similar—"level Lombardy sleeping in its rich transalpine light and resembling, with its white-walled dwellings and the spires on its horizon, a vast green sea dotted with ships."

The Duchy of Milan's social structure was more feudal than that of Florence or Venice. Its great nobles lived with pomp and ceremony, and no name could have been more illustrious than that of Francesco Sforza, Marchese di Caravaggio, the main branch of whose family had ruled Milan until recently. Whether at the marchese's palace in Milan or at his villa near Caravaggio, Fermo ranked after his master in an enormous household. In 1658, while in retirement, a Francesco Liberati, who had served two cardinals and a Roman duke in the same capacity, published his experience of a lifetime in a book entitled *Il Perfetto Maestro di Casa*—"The Perfect Master of the Household"—which gives us an idea of Fermo's duties and social standing.

He must have had more than thirty senior household officers to help him look after the marchese, among them a cupbearer, a seneschal of the dining hall, a steward in charge of the household expenses, a collector of provisions, a storekeeper, and a quartermaster, who organized accommodations. There were also a chaplain, a doctor, and the gentlemen waiting on the marchese at table and in his bedchamber. Then there were the under-servants—butlers, cooks, huntsmen, coachmen, grooms, porters, valets, and footmen. Fermo was responsible for running this vast establishment and engaging and dismissing its members. He paid their wages and bought the food and wine to feed them. Far from being a humble mason, he was the right-hand man of a great Milanese magnate.

We know very little about Francesco Sforza, the marchese himself, but his wife, Donna Costanza Colonna, was a strong and colorful personality, the daughter of Prince Marcantonio Colonna, Duke of Paliano, the heroic captain-general of the papal galleys at Lepanto. Married in 1567, when she was only twelve, she did not at first get on with her husband. She complained to her father, threatening, "If I'm not set free from my lord's house, I'll kill myself, and I don't care if I lose my soul as well as my life." Prince Marcantonio asked the archbishop of Milan, Carlo Borromeo, to intervene, and after moving her to a convent, the archbishop succeeded in reconciling the young couple, and Costanza bore Francesco six children. When her husband died in 1583, she ran the family, now known as "Sforza Colonna," together with its estates, and rescued Fermo's son on more than one occasion, giving him a refuge during the last months of his life.

Since Francesco and Costanza spent most of their time in Milan, Caravaggio may have been born in the city, in the Sforza di Caravaggio Palace, in the parish of Santa Maria della Passerella—"Our Lady of the Footbridge." Brought up here, the little boy would certainly have been very much aware of the Marchesa Costanza.

Located at the junction of the Alpine passes, Milan was as wealthy as Florence or Venice, using rivers, lakes, and canals to export its merchandise. "Milan is a sweet place, and though the streets are narrow, they abound in rich coaches, and are full of noblesse," the diarist John Evelyn recorded in 1646. It must have been like this in Caravaggio's boyhood. Coryate says the suburbs were "as bigge as many a faire towne, and compassed around with ditches of water." Enclosed by a network of canals, notably the Naviglio, which linked it to Padua, its population of over 100,000 was enormous for the age. There were more than 150 churches, many of them magnificent, and a citadel "of an incomparable strength," the Castello Sforzesco.

The duchy of Milan had been ruled by Spain since 1535, through governors who imposed savage taxation. At the same time, a constant flood of gold and silver from Spanish America devalued the currency, so that prices were rising enormously, impoverishing all classes. The regime was deeply unpopular. In April 1572 the governor, Don Luís de Zúñiga y Requeséns, reported to King Philip II at Madrid, "One cannot trust any of the subjects of this state, since many of them are much more sympathetic to France." He was warning Philip that an uprising against the Spaniards might break out at any moment. Even so, Spain was determined to keep the duchy, the expense of a large garrison and the hostility of the Milanese being small prices to pay for its military and strategic advantages. Occupying Milan not only enabled the Spaniards to control the entire plain of Lombardy but it guarded against any threat of a French invasion of Italy from across the Alps.

This was the city of Caravaggio's earliest childhood. When he was five years old, it experienced one of the most terrifying calamities in its entire history.

11

Carlo Borromeo and the Plague, 1576–1578

Tall, painfully thin, with piercing eyes, Cardinal Borromeo was one of the sights of Milan, celebrating Mass in gorgeous vestments at the Duomo's high altar, tramping through the meaner streets to visit the sick and the dying. Accessible to all, he was a father to the city's poor, selling his furniture to feed them, and an uncompromising ascetic who slept on straw and lived on bread and water. His sole luxury was music, in the service of the Church.

Borromeo embodied the new Catholicism of the Counter-Reformation. He has been called the first modern bishop, because he was the first to found seminaries for training parish priests and because he never left his diocese. Besides re-creating the Milanese clergy, he initiated a massive program of church-building all over Lombardy. As Pope Pius IV's nephew, he was cardinal secretary during the last session of the Council of Trent, and he was present on 4 December 1563, when the council issued its edict on the visual arts. Caravaggio must have often heard his parents talking about the saint who played such an important part in the lives of their Sforza patrons, and who fascinated everyone in the city.

As archbishop of Milan, he made many enemies. Alarmed by the extent of his influence, the Spanish governor asked King Philip to remove him as "the most dangerous rebel Your Majesty has ever had," but Philip wisely refused. Borromeo's most violent foes were the Humiliati, a degenerate group of Benedictine oblates, or part-time monks, who lived in scandalous luxury on the vast revenues of ninety abbeys. When the archbishop told them to reform, one of the brethren shot him as he knelt at prayer in his chapel, but the bullet merely grazed his spine, and the Pope ordered the immediate dissolution of the Humiliati.

In August 1576, bubonic plague broke out in Milan, spreading across Lombardy and not coming to an end until 1578. Instead of escaping with the governor and the rich, Borromeo stayed and organized a nursing service and shelters for the sick. He also visited lazar houses, which no one else dared to enter. "He fears nothing," said a Capuchin who knew him. "It is useless trying to frighten him." Convinced that the epidemic was a punishment sent by God, he went every day on processions of atonement, through streets littered with putrid corpses and dying men and women, barefoot, with a rope around his neck and carrying a life-sized crucifix.

Throughout his life, Caravaggio can have known nothing more ghastly than the "Plague of San Carlo," whose symptoms were shivering, shortness of breath, and a sense of unease, followed by a burning fever, purple tumors, and finally delirium. Fermo's family lived in daily fear of being dragged off to a lazar house and ending in a plague pit. There were officials, robed in dingy scarlet, whose job it was to remove the sick and the dead, their carts heaped high with naked bodies and preceded by men who rang bells to warn of their approach. Throughout the stricken city, greasy smoke rose from the bonfires of infected clothes, dirty bedding, and discarded bandages. Houses were nailed up and marked with crosses to show that there were corpses inside. Everywhere was the all-pervading stench of putrefaction.

It was later believed that seventeen thousand died at Milan, and at least another seven thousand in the surrounding countryside. Agriculture and commerce collapsed. No one dared to work in the fields or the shops for fear of meeting the infected. A severe famine broke out. The archbishop sold what was left of his gold and silver plate to buy food for the starving, ordering his servants to make clothes for the naked out of his tapestries.

Many of Fermo's friends and neighbors must have been among the dead. During the summer of 1577 Fermo and his family finally managed to escape to their house at the Porta Folceria in Caravaggio, but the plague followed them. Presumably most of the town's inhabitants ran away to live in the open country, but unfortunately the Merisi were not among them. Fermo died of the pestilence on 20 October 1577, without even time to make a will. Besides his father, Caravaggio lost his grandfather and his uncle, struck down on the same day as Fermo.

Caravaggio was six. All the men in his family had died, suddenly and horribly, after fourteen months of terror. The child can never have forgotten the doleful warning rung by the bellmen, or the sound made by the wheels of the dead cart as it trundled past his parents' house in Milan, or when it came to take away his father's corpse. Death appeared very early in Caravaggio's life. He was shaped by the plague.

Apprenticeship, 1584–1588

Bellori is generally regarded as a key source for Caravaggio's life. He is not always accurate, but he preserves vital information found nowhere else. Born in Rome around 1615, he studied to become a painter, and, when still quite young, joined the Accademia di San Luca, which enjoyed considerable prestige. Instead of pictures, he began to write about artists. In 1671 he became the Accademia's secretary, and when his *Lives of Modern Painters, Sculptors and Architects* was published the following year, it was greeted with applause.

Although he was unquestionably a dedicated scholar, he must be read with caution. "When Michele [Caravaggio] was employed at Milan with his father, who was a mason, while making glue for some painters working on a fresco, he was suddenly seized with a wish to become a painter himself and went off with them, devoting all his energy to painting," Bellori informs us most inaccurately. Caravaggio's father, Fermo, was not a mason, and Caravaggio is known to have at least begun a formal apprenticeship.

When Fermo Caravaggio died, his widow lost her social position and most of the presumably substantial income and perquisites from her husband's post with the marchese. Unable to return to the Maestro di Casa's apartment in the Sforza Palace at Milan, she had to stay at Caravaggio, living on whatever came in from Fermo's small estate. By no means reduced to poverty, she nevertheless found it hard to manage, falling into debt within a few years.

It is reasonable to suppose that, in her straitened circumstances, she was relieved to have Michelangelo taken off her hands and apprenticed to a respectable Milanese painter in April 1584, when he was about twelve and a half. He indentured himself to serve his master for four years, in both his house and his workshop at Milan, paying twenty-four gold scudi. In return, he was to be fed, clothed, and taught the painter's craft.

His master, Simone Peterzano, may have been respectable, but by no stretch of the imagination could he be described as a great artist. Once a pupil of Titian, he ever afterward signed himself "Titiani Discipulus." He had become what art historians call a "late Mannerist." Several churches at Milan still contain his stiff and dreary works with only a faint dash of Titian's color.

Surprisingly, Peterzano's friends included extremely interesting painters. He obtained at least one commission by securing the approval of a genuinely distinguished Mannerist, Pellegrino Tibaldi. Architect as well as painter, Tibaldi had impressed Cardinal Borromeo, who employed him as his favorite church-builder. Among Tibaldi's paintings was a fine *Beheading of St. John the Baptist,* a theme that would one day inspire one of Caravaggio's greatest pictures. Tibaldi may have chosen it because of the cardinal's close links with the Knights of Malta, whose patron saint was the Baptist.

Peterzano was also a friend of the blind Milanese writer and former painter Giovan Paolo Lomazzo, who, in the year Caravaggio was apprenticed, published a book in Milan explaining precisely what Lombard Mannerists hoped to achieve in their painting. Another friend was Antonio Campi, who painted in the "black" manner, emphasizing light and shadow and anticipating Caravaggio's chiaroscuro. The boy could easily have seen Campi's own *Beheading of St. John* at the church of San Paolo in Milan.

One guesses there was a good deal of friction between master and pupil.

Caravaggio had a violent temper. Peterzano came from Bergamo, in Venetian territory, and the Bergamaschi looked down on the Milanese. On the other hand, the inhabitants of the *Contado,* which at Milan meant Bergamo and the Bergamo Alps, were something of a joke among the Milanese. Many came from the mountains to work in the city, or in the plain of Lombardy, and a substantial number had taken over farms abandoned during the French wars. The sophisticated citizens of Milan laughed at them as clodhoppers and bumpkins.

Presumably Peterzano taught Caravaggio to stretch canvases, grind pigments, mix paints, and use beeswax for softening colors. But he never taught him to paint frescoes, which meant painting on a wall with watercolors on wet plaster. Since most of Peterzano's commissions were for frescoes, he must have found his apprentice idle and unprofitable. Later, when frescoes were very much in fashion, Caravaggio nearly starved because his lack of proficiency in this field made him almost unemployable.

Mancini tells us that Caravaggio studied with diligence, if occasionally he did something odd from hot blood and high spirits. Mancini's word *stravaganza* is associated with Caravaggio throughout his career. Bellori, too, believed that when Caravaggio was an apprentice at Milan he worked hard enough, but only at "painting portraits." He seems to have visited picture galleries regularly in an eager quest for ideas. Historians can only speculate on where he went, but it looks as if he traveled as far as Brescia, Cremona, Lodi, and Bergamo.

Bellori was convinced that, as a very young man, Caravaggio had been to Venice, "where he was delighted by the colors of Giorgione, which he copied." He also believed that Caravaggio derived his naturalism from Giorgione, who, in Bellori's opinion, was, of all Venetian artists, "the purest and simplest in rendering the forms of nature with only a few colors." But the accepted view among modern historians is that Bellori's judgment was faulty, because of insufficient knowledge of Giorgione's work, which he had never actually seen himself.

A visit to Venice, which Bellori thought took place when Caravaggio was on the run "after certain quarrels," also seems unlikely. A penniless youth would have had difficulty finding money for the journey, and the earliest sources, Mancini and Baglione, make no mention of such a trip. But Bellori is certainly right about the quarrels. His belief that Caravaggio was "gloomy and quarrelsome by nature" is more than confirmed by Caravaggio's behavior in later life. He may even have failed to complete his apprenticeship. In any case it would have come to an end in 1588. He did not arrive in Rome until 1592, and we have no information about how he spent the four years in between. There are, however, reasonably strong grounds for supposing that he had to leave his native city in a hurry, after a crime that may have been a murder.

IV

The Counter-Reformation

The most important event in Milan while Caravaggio was an apprentice was the death of its archbishop, Carlo Borromeo, in November 1584. The entire population of the city gathered outside the Archbishop's Palace opposite the Duomo, carrying lighted candles and singing litanies. When his passing was announced, such dreadful howls arose from the crowd that observers compared them to the roars of stricken wild beasts. For days afterward, long lines of mourners filed past his bier, thrusting rosaries and crucifixes through the choir railings to touch his feet. Even before the Church canonized him in 1610, Milan kept the anniversary with the solemnities for a saint. He was embalmed and enshrined in crystal in a crypt chapel at the Duomo, which Henry James saw in 1872: "The black mummified corpse of the saint is stretched out in a glass coffin, clad in his mouldering canonicals, mitred, croziered and gloved, glittering with votive jewels. It is an extraordinary mixture of life and death: the dessicated clay, the ashen rags, the hideous little black mask and skull, and the living, glowing splendour of diamonds, emeralds and sapphires."

Carlo Borromeo influenced Caravaggio's art profoundly, although it is most unlikely that Caravaggio ever realized it. At the Council of Trent, the archbishop had been one of the leaders who reshaped Catholicism and harnessed the arts in the service of the Counter-Reformation. He had defined Caravaggio's choice of subjects before he was born, by stressing those that were suitable for a Catholic artist.

The Counter-Reformation was far more than a crusade to save the Church of Rome from Protestantism. It was a revolution within the Church for the renewal of Catholic Christianity. The Council of Trent, which sat between 1545 and 1563, produced a series of extraordinarily influential decrees, dealing with every aspect of life affected by religion. The Counter-Reformation's success in southern Europe, and in much of northern, was assured by the support of the Hapsburgs, the Bourbons, and the Polish kings, who all identified themselves with it.

There is a tradition that the council considered removing all forms of music except Gregorian chant from church services, until the composer Giovanni Palestrina supplied what was wanted. His Masses and anthems were performed constantly at Milan's churches during Caravaggio's childhood and apprenticeship, and at Rome when he was working there. Trent was determined to banish "everything 'lascivious' or impure" from religious art.

Long before the council, during the 1520s, Pope Adrian VI had planned to redecorate the ceiling of the Sistine Chapel because its naked figures scandalized him. Mercifully, he was prevented by his premature death. In 1549 Cirillo Franco complained in a letter to a friend of "that posturing of limbs and all those nudes" in Michelangelo's art. Andrea Gilio's 1564 *Dialogo* against errors in painting attacked contemporary artists for their obsession with the naked body, and criticized them for distorting it in the cause of elegance. He harked back to the time before Michelangelo, urging a combination of the latest technique with true religion, which would produce a purified sacred art. Bishop Franco and Gilio agreed that, as the former put it, "all art in the service of worship should be functional." In the bishop's words, "Everything must be appropriate to its subject."

The fathers of the council trenchantly expressed their decrees. They insisted that it was the duty of all painters to proclaim and explain the truths of the Catholic religion, and, by inference, concentrate on doctrines attacked by the Protestant reformers. In the future, all religious painting and sculpture must stop cultivating art at the expense of devotion. The decrees amounted to a manifesto against Mannerism, rejecting "superfluous elegance," excessive displays of nudity, and paganism.

What gave the council's decrees such force, and ensured that they would have an enormous impact on artists, was the Counter-Reformation's success in bringing about a deep and sustained religious revival. Caravaggio grew to manhood in an age of renewed faith in which, for most people, the redeemed world was more real than the natural. As a result, throughout Catholic civilization, especially in Italy, the decrees were taken very seriously by artists and art lovers. Eventually they would start a cultural as well as a spiritual revolution, with a new art that would one day become known as the Baroque.

An alternative program for painters and sculptors was contained in the preaching of Carlo Borromeo, who emphasized the two Catholic dogmas to which Protestantism was most hostile: good works and transubstantiation, the belief that the bread and wine changed into Christ's body and blood during the Mass. He was equally determined to defend other doctrines rejected by Protestants and stressed the importance of the cults of the Virgin Mary and the saints and of prayers for the dead. Acts of charity and mercy, the Last Supper, the Madonna, and martyrdoms became the proper subjects for painters.

At the same time, the archbishop was eager to see as much beauty as possible in the basilicas of his diocese, which he often rebuilt completely to make them more splendid and impressive. He advocated the most sumptuous pomp for the ceremonies of the Church, and he wanted to adorn his basilicas with noble paintings. No paintings could have been more in accord with the council's decrees than Caravaggio's during his maturity. Despite their occasional brutality, his naturalism and total lack of affectation or of elegance for its own sake were the looked-for response to the decrees' demand for functional art. He seldom used pagan imagery. He seems to have had little interest in the art of classical antiquity. In his later years, his painting was wholly religious. The Counter-Reformation had created a climate to which Caravaggio responded absolutely as an artist.

V

The Flight from Milan, 1592

We do not know why Caravaggio left Milan, but he left as a very young man and never returned. Mancini, in a barely legible note scrawled in his *Considerations,* says that Caravaggio was in a brawl involving "a nobleman and a whore," during which a *sbirro* (policeman) was killed, and that he then spent a year in prison and was forced to sell his patrimony. Bellori seems to confirm the note, writing that "because of some sort of strife he fled from Milan." In his copy of Baglione's *Lives of the Painters* he amplified this, scribbling in the margin that Caravaggio had been forced to escape from the city after killing someone.

Bloodshed was an everyday occurrence in sixteenth-century Milan. The streets were dangerous because they were so narrow. Pious Milanese boasted that by the time Archbishop Borromeo died, crimes of violence had almost ceased in the city. If so, they seem to have been revived very quickly. A man might be robbed or murdered in broad daylight by an ordinary footpad, a starving Spanish soldier, or a *bravo,* one of the hired killers with whom every rich nobleman surrounded himself for his own protection.

Except for lawyers or clerics, any man with the slightest pretension to status wore a rapier and a long dagger. The swarming slum-dwellers also went armed, with knives, which they were ready to use at the least provocation. The ragged, venal *sbirri* (policemen) with their rusty halberds and cumbersome muskets were more of a menace than a safeguard. Much of the violence stemmed from the example set by the Spaniards, the Lombard nobility adopting *hidalgismo,* the outlook of the Spanish aristocrat, or would-be aristocrat, and becoming much haughtier and readier to take offense. Milanese merchants and bankers copied their arrogance, although well aware that a true nobleman regarded anyone connected with trade with the utmost contempt.

Montaigne once observed that everybody went to Italy to learn how to fence. Duelling was fashionable all over Lombardy, especially at the capital. Caravaggio's contemporaries associated a rapier with him as much as they did a paintbrush. Made by renowned swordsmiths, Milanese rapiers were famous. When fighting, a swordsman crossed his fingers round the base of the three-foot blade to guide his aim, the newly invented *botta lunga,* or lunge, giving him an incredibly long reach. Normally a *pugnale,* or dagger held in the left hand, was used to deflect an opponent's blade, but sometimes a cloak was held instead, to whirl into his face.

In November 1588, Caravaggio sold a plot of land for 350 imperial lire, with the option of redeeming it in five years for the same sum. The most likely explanation is that he was out of work, and the widow Caravaggio could no longer afford to support him; judging from what we know of his later years, expensive clothes, gambling, and taverns may have been responsible. In July 1590, and again in March 1591, he and his brother Giovan Battista, the future priest, sold more land, which suggests that the family was increasingly short of money. Apparently the other brother, Giovan Pietro, was dead by now. Their mother died at about the same time. In May 1592, Caravaggio, Giovan Battista, and their sister Caterina divided their parents' estate among them, Caravaggio taking his share in cash. He received 393 lire, which he spent within a very short period, perhaps to pay his jailers. Obviously he kept enough to finance his flight from Milan.

He appears to have left Lombardy toward the end of 1592. The fact that he never went back seems to confirm Mancini's and Bellori's statements that he had to leave quickly after getting into serious trouble with the law. His destination was Rome, and in the document dividing up the family property, mention is made of an uncle, Lodovico Caravaggio, who lived there. But it seems unlikely that he ever intended to live with Lodovico, or that Lodovico wanted him to. According to Baglione, his motive for going to Rome was his wish "to study diligently the noble art of painting." He may also have been encouraged by the knowledge that a fair number of people from Caravaggio had settled in the city, working as artisans, shopkeepers, sword makers, notaries, and papal officials.

The cheapest, quickest, and, on the whole, safest way of reaching Rome was to go to Genoa and travel down the coast by boat. Almost certainly, Caravaggio took this route. He would have gone by felucca, the universal ship-of-all-work until well into the present century. It was an uncomfortable voyage, lasting over a week, probably during autumn or early winter, when the Mediterranean was prone to sudden storms, and wind and rain were commoner than sunshine.

His arrival at Ostia must have been something of an anticlimax. To discourage Muslim raiders, there was no proper port for Rome, and, a day's march southwest, this was the nearest landing place, accessible to only the very smallest ships. Although Ostia had once been the harbor of ancient Rome, it had silted up, so that the town had become a small, miserable village in the middle of a malarial, reed-fringed lagoon. After going ashore, Caravaggio had to travel another fifteen miles over land. At last, he came to the Eternal City and entered through the crumbling gate that, long before, had been the Porta Ostienses but was now the Porta San Paolo.

VI

Rome, 1592

The Rome that became Caravaggio's home was a magic place with its churches, monasteries, palaces, and fountains set amid the majestic ruins from classical times. Only the part next to the Tiber was inhabited. More than half of the ancient city had become a wasteland, often thickly wooded, sometimes interrupted by farms or vineyards. As well as isolated chapels and abbeys and the odd villa among beautiful gardens, there were a few hamlets with cornfields in the southern area. But the overwhelming impression was of a haunted wilderness. Cows and goats grazed beside fallen marble columns, while shepherds folded their sheep in what had once been the atria of Roman mansions, and outlaws hid in noble rooms underground. There was a brooding sense of history and legend.

Some visitors found Rome a melancholy spectacle. "What he had seen was nothing but a sepulchre," the great essayist Montaigne wrote mournfully after his pilgrimage in 1581. But he had to admit that in the grandeur and number of its public squares, the beauty of its streets and palaces, the city was far more imposing than Paris.

The Romans themselves—a mere hundred thousand compared to at least two million in the days of the Caesars—were enormously proud of their past. Antique statuary, constantly unearthed, was purchased eagerly by a host of distinguished collectors, including cardinals, who displayed it in galleries at their palaces and villas. Even humble artisans collected Roman coins. A young tourist from England, Thomas Nashe, grumbled that they "shewed us all the monuments that were to be seene, which are as manye as there have beene Emperours, Consulles, Oratours, Conquerours, famous painters or plaiers in Rome. Tyll this daie not a Romane (if he be a right Romane indeed) will kill a rat, but he will have some registred remebraunce of it." Nashe adds, "I was at Pontius Pilates house and pist against it."

However, the vast majority of visitors, especially artists, seem to have been spellbound by the ruins. During the early years of the century, Raphael and his friends had themselves let down by ropes into the banqueting halls and bedchambers of antiquity, which they called *grotte* (grottoes). By the light of guttering torches they searched for *grotteschi,* their name for Roman murals, gazing entranced at a flickering, phantom world of gods and goddesses, nymphs and fauns.

When Caravaggio arrived, there were also fine modern buildings. Pope Sixtus V (1585–1590) completed the dome of St. Peter's in less than two years, totally rebuilt the Lateran Palace and the Vatican Library, enlarged the Quirinal, built the Sistine Chapel at Santa Maria Maggiore and the Loggia Sistina at St. John Lateran and new streets, notably the Via Sistina and the Via delle Quattro Fontane, besides resiting obelisks and statues all over the city. Less admirably, he demolished one or two important classical buildings but failed in his plan to convert the Colosseum into a wool factory. His greatest triumph was to be the first man since Roman times to construct, or at least restore, an aqueduct in Italy, the Acqua Felice.

Despite his gloomy reflection that Rome was a sepulchre, Montaigne admitted that it had more rich men in coaches than any city he had ever seen. Lesser folk, too, could live very pleasantly. Rising early, they did most of their work in the morning, before dining frugally at twelve—an astonishingly late hour by northern standards—after which they rested till six.

The evening, interrupted by a light supper at about nine, and much of the night were devoted to amusement, in particular to promenading.

The city was especially cheerful during the Carnival before Lent, with pageants and floats, masks and masquerades, cockfights, jousting matches, and battles with sugared almonds (the original *confetti*). Races were run along the Corso by donkeys and buffalo, urged on mercilessly with whips and goads. There were also races by wretched old men and by Jews, who, after being stripped naked, were forced to take part and then pelted with rotten eggs, dead cats, and every sort of filth as they ran. The Corso races always culminated in a wild gallop by fifteen superb Arabian horses.

In its own way, Lent was no less colorful. Brethren from a hundred pious confraternities thronged the streets in hooded gowns of white, red, blue, green, or black, with masks that concealed their faces except for the eyes. On the night of Maundy Thursday, Rome looked as if it were on fire when the brethren marched to St. Peter's in their thousands, each bearing a lighted torch. In their midst were five hundred hooded penitents with naked backs, which they scourged till the blood ran.

On Holy Saturday—Easter Eve—the supposed heads of St. Peter and St. Paul were displayed at the church of St. John Lateran. Given Caravaggio's future obsession with severed heads, he may well have been among the bemused spectators on at least one Easter Eve.

Throughout the year there were more somber entertainments, the most frequent and most popular being public executions. Parents brought their children to watch them, waiting breathlessly for the condemned to receive the Sacrament at the foot of the scaffold and reassure everyone that they were dying reconciled with God. Occasionally heretics—"soul murderers"—were burned, as were sodomites, although they often escaped by paying an enormous fine.

There was also the casting out of evil spirits. Montaigne came across one quite by chance, in the chapel of a church where he had been hearing Mass. A small crowd watched a priest praying over a lunatic bound with ropes, hitting him, spitting in his face, holding a holy candle upside down to make it burn faster, and shouting threats at the devil inside the man. When he stayed crazy and was led away, the priest told the crowd that it was a particularly nasty demon and could be got rid of only by a great deal more prayer and fasting. He then described a more satisfactory exorcism he had recently conducted, driving a really big devil out of a woman; at the moment it left her body, she had vomited up its nails and claws and a large piece of scaly hide. Her friends complained that she was still "not quite herself," but he had explained to them that another evil spirit had immediately entered her, although not such a bad one.

However beautiful Rome may have been, there was always the threat of famine, and even without famine, innumerable beggars and abandoned children starved in the streets. In summer the Romans shivered all too frequently with the ague—malaria from the nearby marshes—and venereal diseases were rife, spread by the many prostitutes who served the bachelor officials. It was an extremely dirty place, its streets filled with human excrement. Almost the only scavengers were the pigs, who roamed everywhere. Despite pleasantly warm weather from spring to autumn, bitterly cold winds set in during the late autumn, followed by drenching rain, which fell throughout the winter.

Rome was notoriously dangerous, even by sixteenth-century standards. If Caravaggio became a violent man, the city's violence and savagery were in some degree responsible. Undoubtedly, there was a peculiarly sinister atmosphere at Rome, and it can have had only a baneful influence on him. Montaigne tells us that it was unsafe to walk through the city's streets at night, that houses were constantly being broken into. Murder was commonplace. More discreet weapons than swords or guns were available. A thin-bladed stiletto, properly handled, caused almost no external bleeding, while a tiny folding crossbow, easily concealed beneath a cloak, was virtually noiseless, even at close range. There was also poison, administered by a quick scratch from a "death-ring," a fruit knife, or a lady's hat pin.

Pope Sixtus had succeeded in making murder less fashionable during the years just before Caravaggio's arrival in Rome, by the most savage measures, but he had died in 1590, and Pope Clement was neither so frightening nor so effective. Gradually, the murder rate rose again. Caravaggio must have seen plenty of heads rotting on the Ponte Sant' Angelo or over the city gates. No assessment of him should omit this background of constant violence and daily executions.

VII

The Rulers of Rome, 1592

Everything in Rome revolved around the pontiff and, after him, the sixty or so resident cardinals. The Papal States were a theocracy governed by priests, and the pope was a temporal prince, an absolute monarch. In 1581 Montaigne saw the then pontiff pass by, wearing a white cassock and a red hat and cape, riding a gray horse decked in red velvet fringed with gold. After him came three cardinals on mules, a hundred mounted men at arms, bareheaded, "each with lance on thigh and in full armor," and then a hundred monsignori and courtiers, also mounted.

When Caravaggio arrived in Rome, the Pope was Clement VIII, only recently elected. A giant of a man, fat and white-bearded, who, from a weakness in his tear glands, often wept uncontrollably, he was kindly by nature, although he prided himself on his severity. He was also prone to fits of undignified rage. The last of the austere Counter-Reformation popes, Clement said Mass every day at noon and confessed every evening to his greatest friend, the Oratorian Cardinal Baronius.

A recent predecessor, the dynamic Sixtus V, had made the papacy stronger than ever. It finally secured undisputed control of central Italy, and Sixtus took advantage of favorable conditions to make Rome very rich. He amassed millions in gold, by draconian reductions in the cost of the papal court and by heavy new taxes on all agricultural produce. Marshes were drained, roads and bridges repaired, farming and manufacture encouraged, all of which would have been impossible before the Spaniards' enforced pacification of the Italian peninsula.

At the same time, the Counter-Reformation was succeeding. The decrees of the Council of Trent were transforming Catholicism, partly because new religious orders were spreading their message, partly because enough Catholics were determined to save their religion from indifference and corruption. Today, it is difficult to appreciate the sheer power of Catholic Christianity in Italy at that period. Only a few rare eccentrics, gathered in swiftly by the Inquisition, ever felt the need or the possibility of doubting the existence of God, even if they criticized the shortcomings of priests or bishops. Science had not yet emerged. There was not even a vocabulary for atheism, while heresy barely existed. Only one or two foreign Protestants were caught from time to time, generally ending at the stake. In any case, it was impossible to be an individual in the modern sense. Well-balanced men and women were convinced that it was neither right nor proper to hold opinions contrary to those of their rulers.

Clement VIII found himself reigning over a Rome much richer and much less threatened than it had been for centuries, leading a Church in many ways reborn. Neither a very clever nor a very forceful man, surprisingly, he was a most successful pope, and especially effective as a statesman. Not only would he receive Henry IV of France back into the Catholic fold, in the face of fierce opposition from Spain, but he used France as a counterweight against Spanish attempts to control him, and he managed to do so without alienating the Spaniards. If the Romans did not love Pope Clement, they certainly respected him.

Next among the rulers of Rome came the Princes of the Church, the cardinals who elected the pontiff and who held all the important offices. Caravaggio must have caught glimpses of them in their magnificent palaces, open to the public; or in their black carriages drawn by black horses; or riding sidesaddle on their mules with the skirts of their long scarlet trains pinned to their bridles. Invariably they were escorted by retinues of violet-clad monsignori and gentlemen in black.

There were also the great lay princes of Rome. Although neither so powerful nor so wealthy as in the past, they were still enormously rich, with splendid palaces at Rome and immense estates in the Campagna. While they usually held some hereditary ceremonial office at the papal court, they were seldom in the city, preferring to stay at one or another of their many castles. Like the cardinals, the princes were surrounded by officials, servants, and hangers-on, so that it would need luck bordering on the miraculous for any of them to take notice of a ragged young painter in search of a patron.

There was a whole host of other clergy at Rome, ranging from bishops to parish priests and seminarians, from abbots to monks and friars. The members of the new religious orders were especially influential. Those who stood out were the Theatines, Oratorians, and Jesuits. There is no record of Caravaggio being in contact with the Theatines, but he saw a good deal of the Oratorians and the Jesuits.

The Oratorians, groups of priests and laymen, preached a cheerful, warmhearted religion, with emotional sermons on the need for simplicity and the value of inner voices. Marching through the streets to prayer meetings in the Catacombs or at some venerated shrine, they sang oratorios, antiphons set to music by composers such as Palestrina or Vittoria. Caravaggio may have come across the *Filippini* as a boy in Milan, where Borromeo gave them an enthusiastic welcome, helping them establish a Milanese Oratory. He may even have seen their founder, Filippo Neri, still alive when he came to Rome, at their church of Santa Maria in Vallicella.

The Jesuit church, the magnificent Gesù, was still being built all through his stay in Rome. With his temperament, he must have been alarmed by the Jesuits' uncompromising discipline but, like everyone else, could not have helped admiring their heroism. They trained their men to welcome death, encouraging them to become martyrs, which was why they commissioned scenes of martyrdom for their churches. The *Spiritual Exercises,* the Jesuit training manual, declared that "no wild animal on the face of the earth can be more ferocious than the enemy in our human nature." It stressed the inevitability of death and brevity of human life. Dying was not to be dreaded but welcomed as the gate of Heaven.

Although Caravaggio received important commissions from the Oratorians and only just failed to secure one from the Jesuits, there is no evidence that he ever belonged to a circle dominated by either order. Even so, he must have heard countless sermons by them; in Counter-Reformation Rome it was impossible to remain unaware of Oratorian and Jesuit ideals. The mature Caravaggio's extraordinarily direct approach when painting, his uncompromising realism, probably owes much more than we realize to the Oratorians.

Both orders were building churches. They required pictures urgently, to proclaim their message. Unfortunately for the young Caravaggio, so far they only wanted frescoes, and he did not know how to paint them.

VIII

The Hack Painter, 1592–1596

When Caravaggio reached Rome, he was penniless. He had brought brushes, paint, and canvases with him from Milan, but, according to Bellori, he could not afford to pay the modest fees charged by the models whom he then thought indispensable. He drifted into the Campo Marzio in the center of Rome, by all accounts one of the city's poorest areas. While sleeping out of doors was not too much of a hardship for a young man during the Roman summer, we know from the Venetian ambassador's dispatches that there was a severe famine in 1593, which began in April and lasted until the harvest. Normally, he could have expected to live on the food doled out to the homeless by religious orders, but because of the shortage of grain this must have been drastically curtailed. He was lucky not to die from starvation.

Fortunately, Monsignor Pandolfo Pucci, an eminent cleric on the staff of St. Peter's, lent him a room. Caravaggio had to pay for it by some kind of work, which he later recalled with a touch of bitterness as "demeaning services," perhaps those of a scullion in the monsignor's kitchen. All he got to eat was a salad in the evenings that, he said with a laugh afterward, "had to do for breakfast, dinner and supper." But, even if Pucci's hospitality was scarcely lavish, it enabled Caravaggio to survive.

The monsignor was steward to a sister of the late Pope Sixtus, whose family, the Peretti, were closely related to the Sforza Colonna. It is more than likely that Caravaggio had written to the Marchesa Costanza, begging for help, and that she had asked Pucci to take him in.

He found time and working space to copy some devotional pictures, which the miserly Pucci admired enough to buy and eventually took back with him to his hometown of Recanati. During this period, Caravaggio also painted the *Youth Bitten by a Green Lizard,* now at Florence, together with a *Boy Peeling a Green Citrus Fruit,* a portrait of the keeper of an inn where he had once stayed, and another long-vanished portrait of which there is no description.

After several months, he managed to leave Pucci, whom he sardonically called "Monsignor Salad," having been hired by Lorenzo Siciliano, who was a hack painter and dealer in cheap daubs. Lorenzo's speciality was mass-producing rough portrait heads, and Caravaggio, so poor that he went almost naked, turned out three heads a day for a few pence each. If any survive, they have not been identified. However, employment at Lorenzo's workshop had one consolation. Another young painter was working there, Mario Minniti from Palermo, who was as poor as Caravaggio. They made friends and lived together for the next few years.

There is no firm evidence for Caravaggio's movements during his early years in Rome, but it looks as if he left Lorenzo's to work for Antiveduto Grammatica, a portrait painter of about his own age who afterward had a modest success with religious themes. At the time, like Lorenzo, Antiveduto went in for mass production. Bellori believed that Caravaggio lived in Antiveduto's house, painting half figures for him. Ironically, in later years, Antiveduto copied his former assistant's mature style, especially the violence. Some of his paintings have been mistaken for lost works by Caravaggio.

Caravaggio moved farther up in the world as an assistant to Giuseppe Cesari, better known as the Cavaliere d'Arpino, one of Rome's most fashionable painters and about to become Pope Clement's favorite artist. He specialized in historical and religious scenes, and, at their best, his paintings were graceful and hauntingly mysterious. It cannot have been easy working for him; he was vain and haughty. Caravaggio probably spent no more than six months in his workshop. During this time, he painted self-portraits with the help of a mirror. One of these, an odd, sickly little *Bacchus* (the *Bacchino Malato*), sits hunched and half naked at a table, holding up a bunch of grapes. His skin is yellowish, his face ugly, with thick lips and would-be mocking eyes. Another painting from this period is the *Boy with a Basket of Fruit,* which has had many highly imaginative interpretations. Some think it depicts autumn, or the sense of taste. Others consider it an allegory of Christ as Love; still others believe it contains a homosexual message. In Bernard Berenson's whimsical view, "The 'Fruit Seller' is a languishing youth in a situation unsuited to his temperament." Whatever the boy signifies, he and his basket of fruit are a magnificent study.

Although Caravaggio did not work long for Arpino, the association ensured his emergence from obscurity. He became known to the city's artists and connoisseurs as a young man of promise. His employer moved among Rome's cleverest and most cultivated men, belonging to the "Academy of those without Senses," whose members pledged themselves as Neoplatonists to forgo sensual pleasure to enjoy more fully the "celestial and divine." Arpino also belonged to the Accademia di San Luca, revived at about this time to improve the status of Roman artists; its cardinal protector was Federigo Borromeo, Carlo's nephew. Some of these discerning minds must have noticed the young Lombard, realizing that if Arpino employed him, he was likely to be talented.

Despite the benefits of being associated with Arpino, Caravaggio developed a lasting hatred for him. Arpino was conceited and overbearing, and nobody ever found Caravaggio easy. Or it may have been sheer envy at the dazzling success of someone still only in his early twenties. Before they could come to blows, Caravaggio left Arpino's workshop in January 1594, after being injured by a kick from a horse. Penniless, he had to enter a free hospital, Santa Maria della Consolazione, which specialized in nursing the victims of street accidents. During what appears to have been a lengthy convalescence, Caravaggio painted pictures for the prior in charge of the hospital, who afterward took them home with him to Spain.

On leaving the hospital, Caravaggio worked with another widely respected artist, Prospero Orsi, a specialist in "grotesques" inspired by the ancient murals he had seen underground. The first documentary evidence for Caravaggio's presence in Rome dates from October 1594, when his name and Prospero's appear as members of a vigil in a church during a "Forty Hours" exposition of the Sacrament. Then he set up on his own, hoping to live by his paintings, but he failed miserably in trying to sell them. To make matters worse, he had to leave a room he had been lent at the Palazzo Petrignani. Once again, he was destitute.

Luckily, some gentlemen of the profession came to his rescue out of pity, and Maître Valentin, a French picture dealer, at last managed to sell some of his pictures. One of them was *The Fortune Teller,* now at the Louvre, which shows a gypsy girl stealing a ring from a young man's finger while she tells his fortune. Caravaggio received a mere eight scudi for it.

This was probably during the autumn of 1596, just before a dramatic change in his own fortunes. Valentin's shop was visited by a distinguished collector, who seems to have admired *The Fortune Teller* but was told that it had already been sold. His attention was drawn to another painting by Caravaggio, *The Cardsharps* (in Italian, *I Bari*—"The Cheats"). During the next century Bellori saw this picture in Cardinal Antonio Barberini's collection and described it: "He depicts a callow youth holding some cards in his hands, with a head which is very well done from life, and wearing a dark suit of clothes, while facing him a young rogue leans on the table with one hand as, with the other behind him, he pulls a false card from his belt. At the same moment a third man next to the youth is reading his cards and signaling what they are to his accomplice with three fingers of his hand. . . ."

The picture disappeared in Paris in 1899 and, long mistaken for a copy, was rediscovered nearly a century later. It is now at Fort Worth, Texas. *The Cardsharps* is just the sort of low-life encounter that Caravaggio must have seen often in the seedy taverns of the Campo Marzio. For his contemporaries, the idea of portraying such a scene was utterly new and startling. The collector who bought it was Cardinal del Monte, who lived at the Palazzo Madama, within walking distance of Valentin's shop, and who was reputed to be one of the most discerning art lovers in Rome.

It is not difficult to guess the excitement in the shop at the sale of a picture to the cardinal. It transformed Caravaggio's prospects. A summons came for him to present himself at the Palazzo Madama. Del Monte then asked him if he would enter his *famiglia,* his household of gentlemen, in *servitu particolare,* that is to say, do him special service as his painter in residence. He would live at the palazzo, and the cardinal would buy his paintings at a fair price. Caravaggio had found the perfect patron.

IX

Cardinal del Monte, 1596

No one could have played a more benevolent role in Caravaggio's life, or one of more vital importance to his development as an artist, than Cardinal del Monte. Seemingly without hesitation, he took the shabby, tricky-tempered young man out of the gutter into his household, where he gave him *parte e provisione,* a room, clothes, and an allowance of food and wine. Del Monte's object was to enable Caravaggio to paint in peace and security. He protected and encouraged him for over four years, even taking in his no less ragged friend Mario Minniti, presumably at Caravaggio's request.

Del Monte is something of an enigma. The official account of his distinguished, if not very eventful, career is in Chacon's massive history of the popes and cardinals, which was published in Rome in 1677. From the comparatively small space devoted to him, we learn that he came from a noble family in Umbria; that he was born in Venice in 1549; and that, as a boy, he had been a brilliant student of classical learning and the law. He had then gone to Rome, entering the *famiglia* of his cousin, Cardinal Alessandro Sforza, and becoming his right-hand man. After Sforza's death in 1581, del Monte entered the service of Cardinal Ferdinando de' Medici, with whom he established a lifelong friendship. When Ferdinando "resigned the Purple" in 1588 on inheriting the grand duchy of Tuscany, he petitioned Pope Sixtus to let del Monte succeed him as cardinal deacon of Santa Maria in Dominica. Consecrated Bishop of Palestrina, and then Ostia, he was dean of the College of Cardinals by the time he died in 1627.

Among his duties was the rebuilding of St. Peter's. He also rebuilt the ruined monastery of Sant' Urbino for a community of Capuchin friars. He was generous to sculptors, painters, and alchemists. "On Sundays, in honor of the Blessed Virgin, he fasted on bread and water, giving alms to the poor," writes Chacon's continuator, and he lived with the utmost frugality, always wearing shabby clothes.

His godfathers had been Titian, the architect Sansovino, and the satirist Aretino, friends of his father, who was a soldier in the duke of Urbino's service. Because of his friendship with Grand Duke Ferdinando, he occupied a Medici palace, representing Tuscan interests at Rome. Essentially a bureaucrat, he was among the poorer cardinals, with an income of twelve thousand scudi but no private fortune. Although as a young man he had flirted with girls and played the guitar, in the puritanical climate of the Counter-Reformation he could scarcely help being austere. Still, his interests were never exclusively clerical. When Federigo Borromeo left Rome, his place as cardinal protector of the Accademia di San Luca was filled jointly by del Monte and Cardinal Gabriele Paleotti, author of a treatise on what sacred art should be in the light of the Council of Trent. His brother, Marchese Guidobaldi del Monte, was a famous mathematician, who had taught Galileo and introduced him to the Medici.

He was also a keen student of alchemy, which was much more than a mere precursor of chemistry. Believing the "divine science" had little to do with magic or making gold, he thought its purpose was to "extract the quintessence of things" and prepare healing elixirs, even if a patient died after taking one. Like Paracelsus, anticipating modern psychologists, he was convinced that a dynamic spirit was at work beneath human nature. Caravaggio, who decorated del Monte's laboratory, may have used alchemical symbolism in some of his paintings. He certainly acquired a smattering of the divine science from his patron, giving his dog the alchemical name of "Raven," a symbol of melancholy—"the bird of Hermes that never rests."

Like all members of the Accademia degli Insensati, Cardinal del Monte was fascinated by Neoplatonism, a philosophy based on the belief that things are more than they seem, and that each possesses an inner reality of its own. It was reflected in the period's taste for emblems, which were intended to alert beholders to hidden meanings within a work of art.

Studies of Caravaggio often credit his complex, subtle patron with homosexual tastes, but their evidence is highly dubious. It consists of no more than a misreading of a report in an *avviso* of 1624 and a single innuendo in the *Relatione della citta di Roma* by Dirck Ameyden, a collection of his *avvisi* that was published in 1642. Handwritten news sheets, the *avvisi* are no more reliable than modern tabloids as historical documents. Pope Clement grumbled that they "spread lies and calumnies."

The report in the *avviso* of 1624 merely says that a cardinal had given a banquet at Palazzo della Cancellari for three other cardinals, including Cardinal del Monte, and for various gentlemen "in the usual fashion." It relates how "for recreation there was dancing after dinner in which the best dancing-masters took part. And because there were no ladies, many youths dressed as women participated, providing no little entertainment." This tells us nothing about del Monte's sexuality.

Dirck Ameyden came from the Spanish Netherlands but was brought up in Rome, where he spent the rest of his life. He claims that del Monte "loved the company of young men, not I think from evil urges, but out of natural friendship." However, Ameyden insinuates rather more by adding that the cardinal hid feelings of this sort until the election of Urban VIII in 1623, when he "indulged openly in his tendencies."

Examination of Ameyden's *avvisi* shows him to have been both untruthful and malicious. The near-contemporary continuators of Chacon's history complained that Ameyden "spoke ill of almost all the cardinals and very unjustly." As a Spanish agent, he was eager to discredit the pro-French Pope Urban and pro-French cardinals like del Monte. His sly reference to del Monte's private life is contradicted by a Venetian ambassador's description of the already aged cardinal in 1617, "a living corpse . . . wholly given up to spiritual exercises, perhaps to atone for the licence of his younger days." Moreover, del Monte himself revealed a taste for girls in a letter written to a friend in 1608, which wistfully recalled their youth together and "all the honeyed moments with the Artemisias and Cleopatras."

There is no whisper of scandal about the cardinal in any other *avviso,* which is significant, since they were notorious for spiteful fantasy. It was a standing joke in Rome that del Monte's friend Cardinal Alessandro Farnese had created the three most beautiful things in the city—the church of the Gesù, the Palazzo Farnese, and "La Bella Clelia," his natural daughter, Clelia Facia Farnese, begotten in the unregenerate days before the Counter-Reformation.

Gossip surpassed itself when del Monte's closest friend, the former cardinal Ferdinando de' Medici, inherited the grand duchy of Tuscany. He was popularly rumored to have poisoned his brother, Grand Duke Francesco, and his sister-in-law, Grand Duchess Bianca. According to one story, Bianca offered a poisoned tart to Ferdinando at a banquet and, after he insisted on his brother tasting it first, she had swallowed a piece in despair. In reality, both Francesco and Bianca died of malaria.

What is beyond question is that Francesco Maria Bourbon del Monte was one of the great patrons of early Baroque Rome. Genuinely benevolent, besides being a lover of the arts, he was a good friend to more than a few struggling artists. Everyone is in his debt for discovering Caravaggio and making possible his career.

X

Palazzo Madama, 1596–1600

Caravaggio spent four years at the Palazzo Madama. His room was no better than a monk's cell, and he probably had to wait on the cardinal at table. Although on the site of the present Palazzo Madama, now occupied by the Italian Senate, the house was completely rebuilt between 1610 and 1642. It was much smaller. From a survey made just before Caravaggio's arrival, we know that it measured sixty by forty feet, with thirteen rooms on the ground floor—"halls, withdrawing rooms, chambers and antechambers."

Caravaggio would have had to pass through three or four rooms before coming to the *salone*. The "cupboard," where gold and silver plate and Venetian glass were displayed, was in an adjoining room, with a buffet from which servants might fetch drink and refreshment. The furniture must have been very sparse, compensating by its magnificence, with gilded leather on the few chairs. The tapestries and hangings were of equal splendor, woven with gold or silver thread. Presumably the house's greatest charm for Caravaggio was the picture collection. Soon his own paintings were hanging on the walls, among them *The Cardsharps,* the *Concert of Youths, The Lute*

Player, a *Bacchus,* and a new version of *The Fortune Teller,* almost certainly commissioned by del Monte to accompany *The Cardsharps.*

As a courtier, Caravaggio lived on an upper floor. According to the survey of 1595, the courtiers' rooms were "in part of wood like friars' cells, with walls at half-height"—cubicles with partition walls that did not reach the ceiling. He dressed in black, receiving two free suits a year. The fashion for black clothes was due to Spanish influence. "Hee is counted no Gentleman amongst them that goes not in black," Thomas Nashe tells us. "They dresse theyr jesters and fooles only in freshe colours."

Historians often exaggerate the comfort of Caravaggio's life at the Palazzo Madama, one writing of "the easy, sybaritic existence that he must have enjoyed in del Monte's palace." In reality, although food, clothing, and a bed were provided, his life was cramped and frugal. They also exaggerate his "friendship" with del Monte, distorting the relationship between patron and protégé in a hierarchic world. There was an unbridgeable gap between a cardinal and a *gentiluomo.* The latter never dared to forget that; if he had certain privileges, he was nonetheless an upper servant.

Francesco Liberati, author of the *Perfect Master of the Household,* had once administered the establishment of an *Illustrissimo.* (Princes of the Church were called *Illustrissimo* instead of *Eminenza* until well into the next century.) He describes how the gentlemen of a cardinal's household waited on him with an elaborate ceremonial, which bordered on the liturgical. They had to keep their hats on while attending him at table, so that they could doff them whenever he drank.

There were, of course, comparatively informal moments, such as the entertainments for Cardinal del Monte's guests, which would certainly have included concerts and plays. We know that the cardinal was very fond of music, especially madrigals, but we can only speculate about his taste in plays. The plays fashionable in Rome during Caravaggio's time in the city included tragedies bloodier than anything in Elizabethan drama. In Giraldi's *Orbeche,* the king of Persia, learning that his daughter has married beneath her, orders the heads and hands of her husband and children to be served up to her at a meal, whereupon she kills both the king and herself. The themes of Speroni's *Canace* are incest and suicide. In Dolce's *Marianna,* the heroine is blinded, her heart torn out and fed to the dogs. Decio's *Acripanda* of 1590 has more horrors than all the rest put together.

It is inconceivable that del Monte's household did not hear regular readings from the *Aminta* and the *Gerusalemme Liberata* of Torquato Tasso, the most popular verse of the day. These two wonderfully elegant poems, one a pastoral and the other an epic, were perfectly attuned to court life, including that of a prince of the Church's *famiglia.*

The earliest known description of Caravaggio dates from July 1597, when he was cited as a witness in an assault case. According to a picture dealer, Costantino Spata, whose shop was near Maître Valentin's, he was small, with a half-grown black beard, bushy eyebrows, black eyes, and long black hair hanging over his forehead. He wore an untidy black suit and torn black stockings, carrying a sword in his capacity as a cardinal's "servitor."

Bellori says Caravaggio was "shown the most famous statues of Phidias and Glykon, so that he would be able to study them." They were, of course, copies, but they could be seen only in the great private collections. The best were at the Palazzo Farnese and the Villa Medici, both of which also contained magnificent paintings. Even if Caravaggio soon discovered, as Bellori suggests, that he had not very much interest in Antique statuary, he must have appreciated the settings in which it was displayed, the enchanting galleries and gardens.

He could stroll in the gardens of the Villa d'Este, the Farnese on the Palatine, the Orsini on Monte Cavallo, the Pincio, and the Aventine, those of the Sforza near Monte Testaccio, those of Papa Giulio at the Vatican, and many more. Fifteen years before, writing of the villas of the great Roman princes, Montaigne had marveled how "all these beautiful arbors are free, open to anybody who wishes to go in, or even to spend the night there with some dear companion, whenever the owners are away, and they are hardly ever in residence." If ever the life of Michelangelo da Caravaggio, as he had begun to call himself, was free from shadow, it must have been during his first springs and summers at the Palazzo Madama. But who were the "dear companions" with whom he may, perhaps, have spent the night in the beautiful arbors?

XI

Homosexual or Heterosexual? 1596–1600

Today, Caravaggio has become a homosexual icon, acclaimed as the greatest of gay painters, a view of him that owes a great deal to the late Derek Jarman's immensely successful film *Caravaggio.* In 1986, in a book about his film, Jarman called the artist "the last sodomite of a dying tradition, parodying Michelangelo and stealing the dark from Leonardo." Jarman was not, however, a historian. No less fancifully, in the film itself, he imagines one pope pawning the dome of St. Peter's, and another arriving at an orgy "dressed as a hairy satyr, wearing the triple tiara."

The historical proof of Caravaggio's homosexuality, Jarman might no doubt have said, lies in his association with Cardinal del Monte, in the "homosexual pinups" he produced for the cardinal, and in never painting female nudes. Others have used these arguments. But del Monte's alleged sexual tastes are demonstrably a myth, while Caravaggio produced at least two female nudes, now lost: *Susannah and the Elders* and a *Penitent Magdalen.* There is also evidence that he had mistresses. So the question has to be asked: Was he really homosexual, or was he in fact heterosexual?

Seventeenth-century ideas about sex were often very different from our own. "The elephant, not only the largest of animals, but the wisest, furnishes an admirable example for married couples," François de Sales wrote in his widely read *Introduction de la Vie Dévote* of 1609. "It is faithful and loving to the female of its choice, mating only every third year, and then for no more than five days." Sexual deprivation was a good thing. At the same time, affections that today would be thought homosexual were considered unremarkable, provided they did not involve sexual activity. Lack of documentary evidence makes Caravaggio's orientation even harder to identify. All we know is what we see in his pictures.

Among his first paintings for del Monte was the *Concert of Youths,* four half-naked young men communicating a secret message. The lutenist is sometimes said to be the artist's friend Mario Minniti, but no proper likeness of him survives, while the horn player may be a self-portrait. One youth has wings, which, with Caravaggio's attempts at classical drapery, shows it is an allegory. Many historians think that the picture represents some aspect of homosexual love. We know from an inventory that the cardinal hung the *Concert* in his gallery, and it has been suggested that Caravaggio was catering for del Monte's homosexual love nest. Yet Baglione, who knew Caravaggio, and probably del Monte too, merely says, "He painted a music party of young men, from nature, and very well."

Another of Caravaggio's pictures for the cardinal was the *Lute Player,* whose model was perhaps a Spanish *castrato,* Pedro Montoya, a member of the Sistine Chapel choir. The boy is so girlish that Bellori thought he was "a lady in a blouse." On the table before him are a violin, a sheet of music, and some figs. The sheet of music reads *Voi sapete ch'io v'amo* ("You know I love you"), the opening lines of a madrigal set to music by Jacob Arcadelt. Yet another painting of an androgynous boy is the *Bacchus* in the Uffizi. Although not among del Monte's collection, it is typical of Caravaggio's work at this stage.

Despite the prettiness of the concert players, it is most unlikely that they were meant to be homosexual pinups. The cardinal would have regarded them as images of platonic love and the transience of earthly happiness. A priest and a member of the Accademia degli Insensati, he probably saw an emphasis on the vanity of this world's beauty, which would awaken sophisticated Christians to a realization of heavenly beauty. In any case, in del Monte's gallery such pictures were heavily outnumbered by Christs, Madonnas, saints, and martyrdoms, together with portraits of the famous down the ages.

No doubt, these so-called pinups look like homosexuals. Yet Caravaggio cannot have been responding to the cardinal's "tastes," which never existed outside the imaginations of a single seventeenth-century journalist and a handful of modern scholars. In the pre-Freudian world of the Baroque, admiration of male beauty did not necessarily mean homosexuality; girlish, Adonis-like looks in a young man were often considered a sign of aristocratic breeding rather than effeminacy. Many of the Davids in Baroque art were pretty enough, and yet most of the artists who created them were heterosexuals. At least one of the youths in the *Concert,* if he really is Minniti, married twice.

There is little evidence, except these early paintings, to suggest that Caravaggio was a homosexual. A vague allegation during a libel action in 1603, for belittling a would-be rival's pictures, was not taken seriously by the court. In 1650, Richard Symonds, an English tourist visiting the Giustiniani collection, was told that the model for the laughing Cupid in *Amor Vincit Omnia* was "Cecco . . . his owne boy or servant that laid with him," but this was mere hearsay. At about the same time, a guide to the Villa Borghese stated that the young David in the Borghese *David and Goliath* was modeled on the artist's "Caravaggino," by implication his boyfriend. This was probably a simple misunderstanding, since David is almost certainly an idealized self-portrait of Caravaggio in his boyhood. Nevertheless, a tradition that he had been a homosexual developed during the later seventeenth and eighteenth centuries.

On these very slender foundations, some modern historians have decided that he had physical relationships with his male friends. "Whether Caravaggio was essentially or exclusively homosexual is far from certain," says Howard Hibbard. "Minniti, with whom he lived for some years, and who may have been the model for the lutenist in the *Concert,* eventually tired of Caravaggio." But the only grounds for suspecting that there may have been a sexual relationship between them was their living together. And even Hibbard concedes that Minniti went off to marry a Roman girl by whom he had a family. He also admits that the homoerotic undertones in Caravaggio's paintings are not necessarily "confessional," accepting that a contemporary story of Caravaggio using a mistress for a model is "not a rumour about a known homosexual."

Caravaggio was strongly attracted by the opposite sex during the latter part of his time at the Palazzo Madama. "Around 1599 he also began to paint women who are desirable in our eyes and were, at least arguably, desired," Hibbard concedes. They would certainly have taken more notice of a cardinal's *gentiluomo* than of some hack painter living in the gutter.

According to Montaigne, Roman women were unusually good looking. "As a rule, the women's faces here are much prettier than those of French women, and you see far fewer uglier ones than you do in France . . . their countenances are stately, gentle, and sweet." If he thought their loose dresses unflattering to the figure, he admired their clothes on the whole. "In raiment they are incomparably more sumptuous than our ladies, everything being covered with pearls and jewels." They kept their distance from the gentlemen, "but during certain dances they mix freely enough, and find plenty of opportunity for conversation and holding hands."

There is nothing to suggest that Caravaggio was ever lucky enough to mix with noblewomen of this sort. Even if, in later years, he was sometimes admitted into the palaces of great Roman magnates, he could not expect to be thought fit company for their wives and daughters, despite being a famous artist. He remained a mere painter. But he met women further down the social scale, and there is every reason to think that he got to know some of them very well indeed. Montaigne thought the Roman courtesans were the most beautiful creatures he had ever seen. No doubt they flaunted their charms before an elegantly dressed young man like Caravaggio. In his black suit and white ruff, carrying sword and dagger, he must have begun to look as if he had money.

The onus of proving what has become very nearly the traditional view, that Caravaggio was a lover of his own sex, rests on its supporters. Their case's most obvious flaw is that the evidence for Cardinal del Monte's allegedly homosexual tastes and his supposed love nest of boys at the Palazzo Madama will not stand up to examination; throughout the cardinal's long career, none of the cardinal's friends or close associates can be shown to have been a practicing homosexual. On the other hand, definite if sparse evidence exists to show that Caravaggio was a lover of women.

Judging from his paintings, it is not impossible that he went through some sort of bisexual phase as a very young man, but as will be seen, it certainly looks as though he was a heterosexual by his midtwenties. In the last analysis, blasphemous as it may seem to our own age, it is quite possible he did not have much interest in sex; he willingly took a vow of chastity when he was in his thirties. Nonetheless, some people will always remain convinced that Caravaggio was essentially homosexual, although their view depends entirely on a subjective reaction to his pictures. A famous German composer, also a homosexual, has claimed, "Of course Schubert was gay—you can hear it in the music." But the majority of Schubert's admirers cannot hear it in the music. Similarly, most of Caravaggio's admirers cannot see it in the pictures, certainly not in his later paintings.

XII

"Nature the only subject fit for his brush," 1596

Although Caravaggio no longer needed to support himself, he worked with ferocious energy. Nor did he have any intention of restricting himself to jeux d'esprit like the *Concert* or the *Lute Player,* produced in unusually sunny moments. A man of many moods, he suffered from the same overriding melancholy as his namesake Michelangelo.

Caravaggio "thought Nature the only subject fit for his brush," says Bellori, explaining that Caravaggio painted *The Fortune Teller* to make the point. He "stopped a gypsy as she was going down the street near his house, and, taking her home, painted her foretelling the future, as is the custom of the Egyptian race." He was, however, by no means the first painter in Rome to reject Mannerism. In 1595 Cardinal Odoardo Farnese, nephew of Cardinal Alessandro, had brought Annibale Carracci from Bologna to work on frescoes at the Palazzo Farnese. Annibale and his two Carracci cousins were so eager to learn from nature that they made detailed anatomical studies of human corpses, while Annibale painted a *Butcher's Shop*. Nothing could be more brutally realistic than the dead and bleeding Christ of the *Crucifixion* with its dreadful wounds, which Annibale took with him to Rome. This gruesome emphasis on Christ's suffering reflects the Tridentine decrees on art, which urged artists to stress the reality of the Gospel story. It is unlikely that Caravaggio did not, at some stage, see Annibale's frescoes and the *Crucifixion*. Ironically, Annibale would one day dismiss Caravaggio's style as *troppo naturale*.

Caravaggio must have been aware of naturalist painters of the past before he heard of the Carraci or saw their work. Now that he was being noticed, he rejected every current artistic theory in a way that many of his contemporaries thought verged on iconoclasm. He painted only what he could see in nature. Yet, like Annibale Carracci, and no doubt unconsciously, he was responding to the Counter-Reformation's demand that simple people be able to understand any religious painting. Even before entering the Palazzo Madama, he had been attempting religious themes. The first example to survive may be the *Penitent Magdalene* at the Doria Pamphili Gallery. Scarcely one of his best pictures, it was admired by Bellori: "He painted a girl sitting on a little chair in the act of drying her hair, with her hands on her lap, and he shows her in a room on whose floor he has placed a little jar of ointment, with ornaments and jewels to signify that she is Mary Magdalene. She holds her head a little on one side, her cheek, neck and bosom being painted in clean, easy, honest colors, their simplicity emphasized by the whole figure's sheer straightforwardness, with her arms covered by a blouse and with her yellow dress pulled up to her knee, revealing a white petticoat of flowered damask." Bellori explains that he has described the picture at such length to demonstrate what a natural style Caravaggio had, and how he had been able to find exactly the right color.

Another of Caravaggio's early religious paintings was the *Rest on the Flight into Egypt,* also at the Doria Pamphili Gallery, which was much admired by Bellori: "An angel stands on one side and plays the violin, while a seated St. Joseph holds open a book of music for him; the angel is very beautiful and, by graciously showing us his profile, displays his winged shoulders and the rest of his naked body, which is partly covered by drapery. On the other side sits the Madonna who, bending her head, seems as though asleep with her baby on her breast."

With its wonderful serenity, this is probably the *happiest* picture ever painted by Caravaggio. The gentleness and tranquility are most moving. Each face is full of kindness, even that of the donkey, whose brown eye is like a great gleaming jewel. The whole composition has been described by the historian Giorgio Bonsanti as "a miracle of peace and quiet." Unaware of the artist's identity, one could imagine that it was the work of a saint. The model for the serene Virgin was the same model who sat for the Magdalene, a not unappealing young woman. Since the *Flight* dates from just before Caravaggio's del Montean period, or from its beginning, she makes an interesting contrast to the so-called "homosexual pinups" from the same period.

Although painted at some time during the first half of Caravaggio's stay at the Palazzo Madama, *St. Francis in Ecstasy,* now at Hartford, Connecticut, was not acquired by del Monte until many years after his protégé had left the *famiglia.* This is surprising in view of the cardinal's close links with the Capuchin Franciscans of Sant' Urbino, and given the likelihood that his friendship with them prompted his choice of subject. Del Monte's delay in acquiring it was probably due to its novelty. Caravaggio seems to have started with the intention of painting St. Francis receiving the stigmata, a miraculous repetition on his own body of the wounds suffered by the crucified Christ. He then appears to have changed his mind. Instead of receiving the stigmata, Francis, portrayed as bearded like a Capuchin, has the wound on his right hand deliberately painted out and is shown swooning in an ecstasy of the sort later associated with Teresa of Avila or John of the Cross. It looks as if Caravaggio was aware of mystical prayer and the *Via Negativa,* the Dark Night of the Soul. The painting is so deeply felt that one almost wonders if it reflects the artist's own experience. And, for the first time, he uses darkness and the chiaroscuro.

What made the *St. Francis* such a novelty was the ecstasy. Although mystical ecstasies were later to become familiar from Baroque representations of St. Teresa (notably by Bernini) and other saints, in the 1590s they were little known, startling, and open to an embarrassing sexual misinterpretation. Caravaggio seems to have been the first to paint this kind of mystical experience. Presumably, it was doubt about the ecstasy's propriety that made del Monte hesitate before adding the picture to his collection. Ironically, while the cardinal saw nothing improper in the *Concert* or the *Lute Player*—both nowadays cited as evidence of homosexuality—and hung them in his gallery, it looks as if he feared the *St. Francis* might cause scandal.

Caravaggio chose a young woman with a strong, beautiful face for his *St. Catherine of Alexandria.* A fourth-century Egyptian martyr, Catherine's executioners tried to put her to death with a spiked wheel, but when it broke, they finished her off with a sword. Here she kneels apprehensively in a white blouse and black velvet dress, her dark blue mantle partly hiding the great spiked wheel, while a martyr's palm lies at her feet. Her large, rather coarse, red hands clutch an elegant sword, not an executioner's clumsy tool but a gentleman's long, slender rapier, designed for dueling. Perhaps it was Caravaggio's own weapon.

The model for St. Catherine was a famous prostitute, Fillide Melandroni, who came from Siena, no mere streetwalker but a lady at the very top of her profession. Often, courtesans were surprisingly pious. According to Montaigne, even if making love, every young whore in Rome would jump out of bed and say her prayers when the Angelus rang. He adds, "These girls are always in the hands of some old bawd, whom they call 'mother' or 'aunt.' "

Fillide posed for another picture. In the *Conversion of the Magdalene*, Mary is magnificently dressed, with sleeves of costly red velvet. She stands in front of a mirror but looks spellbound at her sister, Martha, who rebukes her for her vanity. The Magdalen is about to cover with a cloth the mirror that tells her of her beauty, for it is the moment of conversion. The tension is heightened by strong light and shade. Having been lost for centuries, then found but dismissed as a copy, this picture—now in Detroit—has been widely accepted as genuine.

In the old Roman Missal, the Lesson for the Mass of Mary Magdalen's feast day, taken from the Song of Solomon, contained these words: "Swear to me, then, maidens of Jerusalem, by the wild things that roam in the woods, by hart and doe, that you will not wake my beloved untimely. Hold me close to your heart, close as ring or bracelet fits; not death itself is so strong as love, not the grave itself as love unrequited; the torch that lights it is a blaze of fire." This would have been read out in church, in the simple, easily understandable Latin of the Vulgate.

A year or two later, Caravaggio painted a portrait of Fillide Melandroni as she really was, totally impenitent, *The Courtesan "Phyllis."* Although the picture perished during the destruction of Berlin in 1945, we can see what it looked like from old photographs. No longer posing as a saint, hard, predatory and cheerful, in real life Fillide must have been been recognizable at once as a highly professional prostitute. What is so impressive is the painter's insight into her nature and his ability to convey it.

Despite the lack of interest in classical statuary that so horrified Bellori, Caravaggio's *Narcissus* seems to have been partly inspired by a well-known antique statue of a boy drawing a thorn out of his foot. The artist was far from ignorant of the classics, probably better read than we realize. A crouching Narcissus, his sleeves rolled up, gazes entranced at his reflection in a pool, a boy with a sensual face and loose lips. Some detect a Christian message—know yourself in order to know God. Since its discovery in 1913 by Roberto Longhi, the painting's authenticity has been constantly disputed, but after a recent restoration, bringing back its luminous quality, it has again been generally attributed to Caravaggio.

He produced the occasional still life, though Bellori says "he painted such things with very little pleasure and always felt unhappy at not being able to concentrate on painting people." He once told an enthusiastic patron,

Vincenzo Giustiniani, that as much patience was needed for a really good picture of flowers as for one of people. Several still lifes have been attributed to him, but the only example definitely known to survive is a *Basket of Fruit,* commissioned by Cardinal Federigo Borromeo, who, when he left Rome, took it with him to Milan, where he gave it to the Pinacoteca Ambrosiana. The fruit in the basket is strangely autumnal and appears to have been chosen so as to catch the precise moment when it begins to decay. There are some overripe grapes and figs, an apple with a worm in it, an almost rotting pear, and an aged peach, all placed among spotted, withering leaves. Odd and melancholy, the picture has a wistful, haunting beauty.

Bellori was obviously impressed by another of Caravaggio's still lifes, lost long ago, though he says mistakenly that it was painted for Arpino, when it was almost certainly done for Cardinal del Monte. "He painted a carafe of flowers with the transparency of the water and the glass, and the reflection from the room's window, sprinkling the flowers with fresh dewdrops." Caravaggio may have been inspired by Jan Brueghel, "Flower Brueghel," whose patron was Federigo Borromeo. He could even have met Brueghel, who lived in Borromeo's palace near the Palazzo Madama, and had perhaps seen his own *Carafe of Light,* now at the Villa Borghese.

Caravaggio painted many pictures during his years at the Palazzo Madama, although it is impossible to date any of them with certainty. Others have been lost. Meanwhile, his marvelous talent was beginning to be recognized all over Rome, Cardinal del Monte presumably singing the praises of his brilliant young discovery: "Caravaggio, as he was called by everybody from the name of his birthplace, attracted more and more interest each day by the new colors he was introducing; not as sweet as hitherto, much fewer, dark and powerful, almost as dark and powerful as the blackness he used to throw figures into relief," Bellori records.

> He went so far with this method that he avoided exposing his subjects to the slightest ray of sunlight, but instead placed them in the

> darkness of a closed room, hanging a lamp high up which shone down on the main part of the body in such a way as to leave the rest in shadow, so that it created a truly striking contrast between light and dark. The Roman painters of those days were much intrigued by this innovation, especially the younger ones, who came flocking round him with their congratulations on being "the only imitator of nature."

An important consequence of Caravaggio's revolutionary use of artificial light—candles and oil lamps—seems to have escaped notice. It meant that, unlike other painters, he did not have to depend on daylight and was able to work whenever he wanted. Neither the weather nor the time of day made any difference to him. If he wished, he could paint throughout the night. Yet the really important commissions at Rome continued to elude him because of his inability to produce frescoes. Perhaps to demonstrate that his protégé could produce something better than a fresco, the cardinal asked him to paint a mural in oils on the ceiling of his laboratory, his "alchemy room," in the *casino*, or little house, he owned in the Ludovisi Gardens. The result was "Jupiter, Neptune and Pluto . . . with the globe in their midst . . . placed so that they can be seen from below . . . painted in oils on the vault." This painting, rediscovered in 1969 and identified from Bellori's description, is still intact in del Monte's long-forgotten alchemy room at the Villa Buoncompagni Ludovisi.

XIII

The Year of Murders, 1599

The year 1599, during which Caravaggio's fame and prosperity became assured, was one of high drama at Rome. First, the city suffered a natural disaster. Next, the authorities discovered a tragic murder committed by a noble family. The killing of Count Cenci by his children enthralled the entire city, and the horror of their execution is almost certainly reflected in Caravaggio's painting. The Romans were always thrilled by murders among the nobility, eagerly attending their executions. It is most unlikely that Caravaggio was absent from the huge crowds that watched the Cenci die, since his patron, Cardinal del Monte, had been asked by Grand Duke Ferdinand to try to secure a reprieve for them. For months, the Palazzo Madama must have talked of nothing but the Cenci case.

Romans have never been strangers to winter rain. Even so, when the Tiber suddenly burst its banks on Christmas Eve 1598, they were caught off guard. By Christmas morning, much of the city was flooded and strewn with debris, with several low-lying districts under water that was still rising. The inhabitants of many of the houses around the Castel Sant' Angelo and in Trastevere took refuge on their roofs. There were no Christmas services in the churches, not even in St. Peter's, and Pope Clement wept unceasingly.

Nor was there any flour or bread, since all the flour sacks in the city's cellars had been spoiled. When the water went down two days later, fifteen hundred bodies were found in the streets, some washed in from the countryside. Early in the new year, the rain returned, heavier than before, while, because of warm winds in the mountains, melting snow flowed into the Tiber. On 8 January 1599, the river burst its banks again, and everybody fled to the high ground. Even the pope left the Vatican to take refuge in the Quirinal. But at last the waters receded, the debris was cleared, and normal life resumed.

On the day before the second flood, a young noblewoman, Beatrice Cenci, had been arrested with her stepmother, Lucrezia, and taken to the dungeons of the Castel Sant' Angelo. Her brothers, Giacomo and Bernardo, were already in the Tordinona Prison, under suspicion of having murdered their father. Count Francesco Cenci had been ruined by paying a fine of one hundred thousand scudi, to avoid burning at the stake for sodomizing his stable boys and servant girls, besides beating them till the blood flowed. He had also beaten his sons and his daughter, Beatrice, the latter with a broomstick. To economize, he had moved from Rome to the mountaintop castle of La Petrella, on the Neapolitan border, taking Beatrice and his second wife, Lucrezia, with him, and virtually imprisoning them. Several times he raped Lucrezia in front of his daughter, and on one occasion he tried to sodomize his fifteen-year-old stepson. When the women attempted to escape, he thrashed Lucrezia with a cudgel and Beatrice with a bull's pizzle. His daughter found an ally and a lover in the castellan Olympio Calvetti, who was wanted at Rome for murder, while her brother Giacomo sent opium. In September 1598, after being drugged by Beatrice, Count Francesco was killed by Olympio and the coachman Catalano with a hammer and a rolling pin. His body was thrown off a wooden gallery into the courtyard below; a railing was broken to make it look as if he had fallen down accidentally and died in the fall. But the suspicious villagers alerted the authorities. When the Cenci came back to Rome in December, they were placed under house arrest, Pope Clement himself asking to be kept informed of the investigation's progress. The *avvisi* reported regularly and colorfully about the case. Stories circulated all over Rome about the victim's disgusting misdeeds, and it was generally agreed that he had deserved to die.

There was also another much talked of murder case in Rome in early summer 1599. Marcantonio Massimi belonged to the most august of Roman princely families. He and his brothers had already escaped the scaffold, despite having killed their stepmother. A beautiful peasant, Eufrosina Corberio, she had been the mistress of one of the Colonna, who murdered her husband to get her. He then passed her on to Marcantonio's widowed father, who grew so infatuated that he married her. Enraged at their mother's replacement by a low-born whore, Marcantonio and his four brothers called on Eufrosina early in the morning after her wedding in 1585 and shot her as she lay in bed. Only one of them, Luca Massimi, was ever brought to trial for her murder, and he was speedily acquitted on the plea that he had been avenging the family honor. Luca was murdered in 1599, poisoned by Marcantonio; the other brothers were already dead, and he wanted to inherit their father's estate undivided. Falling under suspicion at once, he was imprisoned in the Tordinona, where, under torture, he confessed. On June 15 he was executed in the small piazza in front of the Ponte Sant' Angelo, comforted, we must hope, by Pope Clement's "holy benediction."

Marcantonio Massimi appears to have been hanged. Montaigne has an account of such a hanging. A huge crucifix, draped in black, preceded the cart that took the condemned man to the gallows. On the way, he continually kissed a picture of Christ held up to him by two members of the Confraternity of St. John the Beheaded. "At the gibbet, which was a beam between two posts, they held up this picture before his face till the moment he was thrown off the ladder. He died as criminals usually do, without a struggle or a cry . . . and after he was dead they cut his body into four quarters."

Marcantonio had no obvious links with the Cenci. But when Andrea Caproni, a member of the Duke Cesarini's household, was arrested in August for "inflicting wounds on his own brother," it was rumored that Caproni had been imitating the Cenci. Early in September, the Cenci's cousin, Paolo di Santa Croce, was arrested at Subiaco after murdering his mother in her bed for refusing to leave him her estate. Outraged, the pope insisted that Paolo must die.

The Cenci's final interrogation took place in August, all being tortured with the *strappado*. Arms tied behind the back, each was hoisted off the ground by a rope, dislocating the arms, then lowered, the limbs reset and the process continued till he or she confessed. Beatrice stubbornly refused to admit her guilt or incriminate her family, claiming that the entire murder had been Olympio's work, since she knew that he had recently been killed by bounty hunters for the price on his head. She confessed only when she saw that there was no point in further denials. The duke of Modena's agent reported, "The case has touched the heart of everybody in Rome, especially the fate of the girl. Not yet eighteen, she is of great beauty, with the most graceful manners, and very rich, with a dowry of over 40,000 scudi. She showed such extraordinary courage under torture that all were amazed."

The executions took place on 11 September. By dawn, the Castel Sant' Angelo's battlements were packed with spectators, as was every window or rooftop in sight of the bridge of Sant' Angelo. Most of the spectators seem to have come in a mood of pity, lamenting, "Poor folk, poor wretched creatures, poor unhappy people." At about nine-thirty A.M. a procession of officials, clergy, *sbirri,* and pikemen emerged from the Tordinona, escorting two open carts. Giacomo Cenci stood in the first, stripped to the waist, his eighteen-year-old brother, fully dressed, in the second. As they went, an executioner tore Giacomo's naked trunk with long, red-hot, iron pincers, methodically ripping out muscles and tendons, but he did not utter a sound. En route, the two ladies joined the procession, walking at the head. Lucrezia, "a shaking rag," had to be supported. Beatrice was very calm.

A machine like a primitive guillotine stood on a scaffold at the end of the Ponte Sant' Angelo. Lucrezia had to be carried up the ladder, fainting before the blade took off her head with a single stroke. Beatrice needed no one to help her, climbing up briskly and laying her head down without any fuss. When the blade dropped, a great wailing broke out among the crowd. Giacomo followed, bleeding from every pore of his mutilated body, to be *mazzolato*, clubbed to death with a mace. The first blow splintered his skull, then the executioner removed his head with a knife, cutting his body in four with an ax and hanging the quarters from hooks at the edge of the scaffold. Young Bernardo, deliberately left unaware that he was not to die too, fainted during each execution before being led off to become a galley slave.

When night fell, the Cenci were taken away for burial by brethren of the Confraternity of St. John the Beheaded, each to a different church. The hooded brethren lit the way with lanterns whose windows were painted with their device, the head of St. John the Baptist on a charger. A huge crowd followed Beatrice, carrying torches. When her bier was set down in the church of San Pietro in Montorio, "until midnight all the populace hastened there to weep over the corpse and place lighted candles around it." Flowers were showered on the beautiful head.

It is hard to believe that Caravaggio would have stayed away from the Cenci's execution, did not see their corpses exposed to public view by the Ponte Sant' Angelo, or did not watch the brethren of St. John escorting them through the night on their last journey, with the Baptist's head glowing on the lanterns.

XIV

The First Severed Heads, 1599

In Caravaggio's Rome he could scarcely avoid seeing public executions. Almost daily, proclamations announced, "Today there will be hangings, quarterings, and clubbings." There were nearly as many beheadings. He was well accustomed to watching condemned men and women being led in chains through the streets to the scaffold. Perhaps he knew that during the condemned's last night on earth priests often howled like demons in rooms over their cells, rattling fetters in the hope of conjuring up thoughts of hell and arousing a wish to die in the penitent.

But only now did Caravaggio start to paint severed heads. Historians date the earliest of these disquieting pictures to sometime during the last two years of the seventeenth century. There is no direct evidence that it was at the end of 1599, yet arguably what had been done to the Cenci at the Ponte Sant' Angelo first inspired him.

The poetry readings at the Palazzo Madama, or in any other great Roman household, must have included descriptions of decapitation. Sixteenth-century poets had seen plenty of beheadings. In *Orlando Furioso* Ariosto describes the death of the monster Orrilo, whose limbs had an alarming knack of rejoining his trunk after they had been severed. Having cut off his head, under the delusion he has triumphed, the hero Astolfo rides away with it, but:

The stupid monster had not understood
And in the dust was groping for his head

Astolfo realizes his mistake just in time, learning that Orrilo can be killed by destroying a magic hair on his head. He shaves the monster's skull and ensures a happy ending.

It is clear to anyone who looks at Caravaggio's paintings that he was unhealthily fascinated by decapitations, especially those in the Bible. The first beheading he painted did not, however, come out of the Bible. It was, to use Baglione's description, "a really frightening Medusa with vipers for hair, set on a shield." The Medusa was one of the Gorgons, the three fearsome maidens from Greek mythology, with hissing serpents instead of hair and brazen claws instead of hands. She possessed a face so terrifying that anyone who looked upon it was turned to stone. To kill her, the hero Perseus had to use a mirror, so that he could cut off her head without looking at her face.

The picture is painted on a leather shield. Blood drips from the head of Medusa, who shrieks in horrified disbelief, her eyes protruding in anguish. Bernard Berenson commented that it was very like the photograph of a head he had seen, taken "the instant after its owner was guillotined." What makes the Medusa still more unnerving is that she may be a self-portrait of the young, clean-shaven Caravaggio. Despite its macabre quality, Cardinal del Monte valued the shield so highly that later he sent it as a gift to his illustrious friend the Grand Duke Ferdinand, at Florence, where it remains today in the Uffizi.

Judith and Holofernes was painted at about the same time as the *Medusa.* Judith was a Jewish heroine who saved Israel from the Assyrians by decapitating their general, Holofernes, as he lay in his tent in a drunken stupor. The Book of Judith relates how: "she took him by the hair of his head, and said 'Strengthen me, O Lord God, at this hour.' And she struck twice upon his neck, and cut off his head, and took off his canopy from the pillars, and rolled away his headless body. And after a while she went out, and delivered the head of Holofernes to her maid, and bade her put it in her wallet."

As his model for Judith, Caravaggio employed the prostitute Fillide Melandroni, who had sat for *St. Catherine* and for the *Conversion of the Magdalene*. Brows bent in fierce concentration, her strong, handsome face wears a look of disgust and savage concentration as she hacks off the Assyrian's head with a hunting sword, the only sword a sixteenth-century lady would have been accustomed to handling. Holofernes screams in agony, a stream of blood spurting out as the blade slices through his neck. His contorted face is almost certainly a self-portrait of the artist, bearded by now. Judith's maid, standing next to her mistress, holds a bag in which to put Holofernes's head. An old crone, bald and toothless, her face is disfigured by huge wrinkles. For all the horror of the scene, there is something slightly comical about her—she is very nearly a caricature.

Judith and Holofernes is much more alarming than the *Medusa.* A somewhat questionable eighteenth-century source claims that when pressed to comment on the picture, Annibale Carracci replied, "I don't know what to say, except that it is too natural." If Carracci really did say this, perhaps it was because he was repelled by the brutality that, to a modern observer, seems to verge on sadism or sado-eroticism. One has the inescapable impression of an almost gloating enjoyment of the cruelty. However, Caravaggio's motives involved much more than sadism.

There was a very famous *Judith and Holofernes* in Rome, of which Caravaggio cannot have been unaware, Michelangelo's painting on the ceiling of the Sistine Chapel, in which Holofernes's head was a self-portrait of Michelangelo. It has been suggested that Michelangelo was identifying himself with evil, publicly confessing that he was a sinner. Similarly, it has been argued that in later self-portraits of himself, such as that of Goliath beheaded by David, Caravaggio was announcing to the world that he was a sinner.

Certainly, at that date it was far from unknown for artists to depict themselves as penitents.

By the time he died, he had painted a dozen severed heads, some of them unmistakable self-portraits. Contemporaries appear to have found nothing odd or morbid in this fascination with beheading. Mario Minniti even copied him, painting a *Judith and Holofernes* of his own. According to some modern historians, it was an obsession that stemmed from a subconscious fear of impotence, but this does not tell us very much about what went on in his mind. And the more one learns about Caravaggio, the more one realizes he was never simple or straightforward.

Alchemy may provide part of the answer. "Beheading is significant as the separation of the 'understanding' from the 'great suffering and grief' which nature inflicts on souls," explains Jung in *Mysterium Coniunctionis,* citing alchemy texts. He adds that, for alchemists, the head was the abode of the understanding and the soul. While it is too much to suggest that Caravaggio was painting an alchemical statement of his search for wholeness, he must have been well aware of alchemical symbolism. We shall never know why decapitation figured so often in his art. All we can be sure of is that it reflected some hidden anguish.

XV

The Contarelli Chapel, 1599–1600

Suddenly, Rome realized that Caravaggio was one of the great painters of his age. Once again, del Monte had intervened decisively in his career. Through the cardinal, Caravaggio secured a really important commission, of a sort that had so far eluded him: to decorate the side walls of a chapel in the church of Rome's French colony, San Luigi dei Francesi. The chapel was named after the cardinal who had bequeathed money for this purpose, Matthieu Cointrel, in Italian, Contarelli. Arpino had originally been engaged to fresco the walls, but for some reason had not done so. Angered by the delay, the clergy in charge of the church tore up the contract with him and invited Caravaggio to decorate the walls with pictures of the martyrdom of St. Matthew and of his calling by Christ. Presumably after he had submitted satisfactory sketches, on 23 July 1599, a new contract was drawn up, in which he undertook to paint both for four hundred scudi, the amount asked by Arpino. It is not clear from the contract whether the clergy understood that he was going to give them paintings on canvas instead of frescoes, but it is likely, since del Monte knew that he never painted frescoes.

It was highly flattering for Caravaggio to replace the most fashionable painter in Rome and command the same fee. Even so, it must have been a daunting commission. He had never before painted such vast pictures, in which the figures would have to be life-sized. The year 1600 was a jubilee year at Rome, which must have inspired a sense of urgency among the clergy of San Luigi de' Francesi and may explain why they replaced Arpino by Caravaggio. There were very good grounds indeed for Baglione's jealous suspicion that del Monte ("*his* cardinal") had helped them make up their minds, since he was a member of the Fabbrica of St. Peter's, which controlled the fund left by Contarelli. Starting late in 1599, Caravaggio finished by midsummer the following year.

Fortunately, both *The Martyrdom of St. Matthew* and *The Calling of St. Matthew* are still at San Luigi dei Francesi. "Because of the darkness in the chapel and their color, these two paintings are not easy to see," Bellori commented. However, Caravaggio exploited the chapel's gloom to create a chiaroscuro of dramatic contrasts between dark and light, making his pictures all the more startling.

Bellori described the *Calling:* "He painted several of the heads from life, among which is that of the saint, bending down to count his money, but with a hand on his breast and turning toward the Lord. Near him an old man puts his spectacles on his nose, watching a young man who pushes the money toward him to where he sits at the corner of the table." The picture startles by its realism, and Berenson thought it resembled a police magistrate's arrival at a gambling den, "like the illustration to a detective story." Yet the scene is moving and deeply spiritual, dominated by the shadowy, mysterious Christ, who calls Matthew with a majestic gesture.

The other painting, the *Martyrdom,* is no less flippantly dismissed by Berenson. "An elderly man lying on the escarped edge of a pit, presumably in the vaults of a prison, is seized by a slender nude with a drawn sword. . . . The startled onlookers scatter, while a child dives down from above with a palm in his hand." This is not too bad a description, but there is much more to the composition. Caravaggio took the story from *The Golden Legend,* a collection of the lives of the saints first compiled by Jacobus de Voragine in the thirteenth century. It recounts how, after having apparently been converted to Christianity by St. Matthew, King Hyrcanus of Ethiopia ordered his execution when he reproached him for keeping two wives. Hyrcanus's face is at once gloating and compassionate as he sees him being killed. What makes the face fascinating is that it is a self-portrait, perhaps reflecting how Caravaggio felt when he was a spectator at the death of the Cenci. An X ray of the *Martyrdom* has revealed that at some stage the artist altered the composition drastically, painting in what became his normal manner, directly onto the canvas without any preliminary drawing.

The *Calling* and the *Martyrdom* caused a sensation when they were unveiled at San Luigi dei Francesi in July 1600. Both were acclaimed. Baglione concedes, "This commission made Caravaggio famous," but he also claims that ill-natured people, especially those who disliked Arpino, went out of their way to "overpraise" the paintings, to upset established artists.

"Because Caravaggio put an end to dignified art, every artist did just as he pleased, destroying all reverence for Antiquity and for Raphael," Bellori grumbled half a century later. "Now began the depiction of worthless objects, a preference for filth and deformity . . . the clothes they paint are stockings, breeches and shaggy caps, while in their figures they show only dead skin, knotted fingers and limbs twisted by disease." Predictably, the Victorians shared this aversion. Caravaggio had "resolved to describe sacred and historical events as though they were being enacted in the Ghetto by butchers and fishwives," wrote John Addington Symonds. "His martyrdoms are inexpressibly revolting, without appeal to any sense but savage blood-lust."

However, more Romans approved than disapproved. He was elected to the prestigious Accademia di San Luca, while younger painters began to hero-worship him, and there were offers of valuable commissions. He had already signed a contract in April 1600 with a Siennese gentleman for a large painting, which he finished by November, receiving two hundred scudi. Nothing else is known about this picture, or about the person who commissioned it.

Meanwhile, throughout 1600, the Church provided a helpful background in Rome for the display of Caravaggio's paintings. On Ascension Day 1599, Pope Clement announced that the coming year would be a "jubilee" or "holy year," when indulgences could be obtained at Rome by anyone who confessed, did penance, and received Communion. On Christmas Eve he went in procession to the portico of St. Peter's, where a great crowd of worshipers was waiting outside. One of the five doors opening from the portico into the basilica had been bricked up and adorned with a gold cross, the "Golden Door." After praying and reading from the Scriptures, the pope descended from a throne in front of the door and knocked on it with a silver hammer. Having been cut away from its jambs and lintels, the door fell in at once; it would be closed again on the following Christmas Eve. Sprinkling the doorway with holy water, Pope Clement, bareheaded and carrying a torch, processed to the high altar and began chanting the first vespers of Christmas Day. At the same time, the other doors were opened and the waiting crowd poured in. Cardinals conducted similar services at each of the seven "pilgrimage basilicas," and Caravaggio's duties may have included attendance on del Monte at a service of this sort.

All public amusements were banned. An almost Lenten austerity prevailed. From innumerable pulpits, preachers harangued the pilgrims who had come from all over the Catholic world, reliably estimated at over a million during the year. This was the somber atmosphere in the city when the *Calling of St. Matthew* and the *Martyrdom* were unveiled in the Contarelli Chapel.

The year also saw the execution of the Neoplatonist heretic Giordano Bruno. The archives of the Confraternity of St. John the Beheaded relate how in February 1600, "fixing his brain and mind in a thousand errors and vain conceits, he remained altogether stubborn while being taken by the officers of justice to the Campo dei Firoi where, after being stripped naked and bound to a stake, he was burned alive. Our brethren sang litanies throughout, begging him until the very last moment to conquer his obstinacy.

And so ended his agony and his miserable life." Caravaggio may not have even noticed Bruno's burning, although the Campo dei Fiori was the city's main shopping center. An obscure, runaway friar from Naples did not stir the imagination in quite the same way as did Beatrice Cenci.

While Giordano Bruno may have been a hero to Victorian freethinkers, to those few of his contemporaries who knew anything about him, as an atheist he was no better than a lunatic. Sane men believed; conformity was considered to be in no way mediocre or stultifying. Most of the period's great artists were devout, practicing Catholics; Rubens, Guercino, and Bernini, for example, generally went to Mass several times a week, spending long hours in prayer. And Caravaggio himself was to join a religious order.

The coincidence of Bruno meeting his death in the year of Caravaggio's first triumph underlines the artist's commitment to the Christian faith. Despite being a rebel by temperament, he was passionately orthodox in his religious beliefs and never in trouble with the Inquisition. One has only to look at his paintings to realize that he totally rejected Neoplatonism and ideal forms, let alone heresy or witchcraft. Essentially a Catholic of the Counter-Reformation, after the Contarelli Chapel he produced few secular pictures, and during the crises of his later life he chose religious themes, generally from the New Testament, as an outlet for his emotions. When he painted light, it symbolized the light of the Gospel, while the timeless quality of his art came from prayer and meditation.

Undoubtedly, 1600 was a turning point for Caravaggio, and the man who had made his fortune was Cardinal del Monte. Yet he decided to leave the cardinal, moving out of the Palazzo Madama in the late summer or early autumn of the same year. Probably he found life in del Monte's household too restrictive and uncomfortable, and the cardinal, who was not rich, paid him comparatively little for his pictures. By now, Caravaggio could afford to do whatever he wanted; he was beginning to secure lucrative new commissions from wealthy new patrons.

XVI

The New Patrons, 1600–1602

When Caravaggio left the Palazzo Madama, the brothers Cardinal Girolamo Mattei and Marchese Ciriaco Mattei invited him to live in their house, now the Palazzo Gaetani. They belonged to a rich and distinguished family of the city's old nobility, supposedly descended from the ancient Roman hero Mucius Scaevola. But although he was cardinal protector of Ireland, like del Monte, Girolamo was only one of the minor cardinals. Both he and Ciriaco were enthusiastic art lovers. Their initial interest in Caravaggio was probably aroused by the fact that the Mattei Chapel in the church of the Aracoeli was dedicated to St. Matthew, the family patron. During the 1580s, a fresco in the chapel by Girolamo Muziano, *The Martyrdom of St. Matthew,* had anticipated Caravaggio's painting at the Contarelli Chapel. He may have inspected it while working on his own version, and quite possibly his visit brought him in contact with the Mattei.

At some time during 1600–1601, Ciriaco Mattei ordered a *St. John the Baptist* (later known as the *Pastor Friso*) from Caravaggio, as a gift for his son, Giovan Battista, a picture of a cheerful, naked boy embracing a sacrificial ram. In January 1602, Ciriaco paid for a painting originally called *Our Lord at the Breaking of Bread,* which is now the *Supper at Emmaus* in the National

Gallery in London. What made this so unusual was the beardless Christ, reflecting the interest recently shown in early Christian art by many leading churchmen, especially by Cardinal Baronius.

The following January, the marchese made another payment to Caravaggio for a *Taking of Christ,* much praised by Bellori, who particularly admired Judas giving the treacherous kiss and the soldier in armor seizing hold of Christ. (It was found in a Jesuit house in Dublin in 1990.) According to Baglione, Ciriaco Mattei also bought "St. Thomas who pokes his finger into the Saviour's ribs," now in Berlin, a gruesomely realistic portrayal of the Doubting Apostle's moment of truth.

Baglione comments, with barely disguised envy, that Ciriaco Mattei had succumbed to stories of Caravaggio's genius spread by his friends, so the artist was able to extract hundreds of scudi from the marchese. However, the artist's most important patrons were undoubtedly the Giustiniani brothers.

Vincenzo Giustiniani, born in 1564, was a Genoese from the former Genoese colony of Chios, who, after its conquest by the Turks, had settled in Rome. His elder brother, Cardinal Benedetto Giustiniani, was papal grand treasurer, and he himself banker for the apostolic camera. A Jesuit, but also a friend of the Oratorians Filippo Neri and Baronius, and with an uncle, Cardinal Vincenzo Giustiniani, who was General of the Dominicans, Benedetto had far more influence than Francesco del Monte. He was also much richer. Although the Marchese Vincenzo was married, with a family, the brothers shared a palace almost next door to the Palazzo Madama, and were obviously on friendly terms with their neighbor.

Normally the Genoese were unpopular at Rome. They had spread all over Italy and were disliked everywhere as bankers, moneylenders, and tax collectors who bought titles and estates at knockdown prices, fawning on the Spaniards to such an extent that they were called *meretrici di Spagna*—"Spanish whores." However, if the old Roman nobility may secretly have regarded the Giustiniani brothers as wealthy upstarts, they could not help being impressed by the way they spent their money. Benedetto and Vincenzo shared the same tastes, filling their palace and their villa in Bassano Romano, which contained a private theater, with paintings and classical statuary. Benedetto was particularly fond of such artists as Jan Brueghel, Gerrit van Honthorst, and Luca Cambiaso, a fellow Genoese.

Clearly, both brothers were keen admirers of Caravaggio's painting, eventually acquiring fifteen pictures by him, including six portraits. It has been suggested that Benedetto commissioned the religious works and Vincenzo the profane. Whatever Baglione may say about Ciriaco Mattei having bought the *Incredulity of St. Thomas,* it appears to have been one of the religious works painted for Benedetto. The Giustiniani did more than buy his pictures, they urged other Roman patrons to employ him.

In a contract of September 1600 for a *Crucifixion of St. Peter* and a *Conversion of St. Paul*, Caravaggio was given a banker's order drawn on the Marchese Vincenzo Giustiniani, but the pictures were to be painted for Monsignor Tiberio Cesari, Pope Clement's treasurer, who had bought a chapel in the church of Santa Maria del Popolo and commissioned Annibale Carracci to decorate it. Vincenzo insisted that he use Caravaggio as well. In the *Crucifixion of St. Peter,* Peter is a fine old man with a bald head, showing complete indifference as the cross to which he has been nailed is raised upside down by three brutish executioners; from his reflective face, he is apparently remembering how Christ suffered the same death. In the *Conversion of St. Paul,* the apostle lies flat on his back, blinded by the vision and raising his arms to embrace it. Above him stands his patient horse, held by a groom, both unaware that anything is happening. The vision is conveyed by an explosion of dazzling light, signifying the presence of God. An earlier version of the painting in the Odescalchi Balbi collection is not so successful, although it has the same marvelous light.

Generally, light was the only symbolism Caravaggio employed. It had an essentially spiritual meaning for him, that of the "light shining in the darkness" of St. John's Gospel. He used it for evoking holiness, the light of heaven as opposed to the darkness of hell, and did so very movingly in his *Taking of Christ.* He also used it to signify inspiration, as in his portraits of St. Matthew and St. Jerome. But nowhere did he use light more effectively than in the *Conversion of St. Paul* at Santa Maria del Popolo.

Another commission was for the Discalced (Barefoot) Carmelites' church of Santa Maria della Scala, where Laerzio Cherubini, a rich lawyer, had bought a side chapel. His professional activities having brought him into contact with Cardinal Giustiniani, he probably chose Caravaggio on the Marchese Vincenzo's advice. In a contract drawn up in June 1601, Caravaggio agreed to paint a *Death of the Virgin* for an initial payment of fifty scudi, with the proviso that Vincenzo should decide the final price, which was the unusually high sum of 180 scudi. The most likely date for its completion is between November 1601 and June 1602.

What he painted may seem strange to modern Catholics, accustomed to the dogma of the Virgin's bodily assumption into heaven. He shows her as a corpse that has fallen asleep in the Lord, what the Orthodox Church calls the "Dormition." At the time, it was in full accord with Catholic teaching. The Virgin's deathbed is surrounded by grieving apostles, with a bowed Mary Magdalene seated in the foreground. This is a true portrayal of death—one can feel the sense of shock and loss among those who had loved and cherished her. She is painted with stark naturalism. Hers is an exhausted, swollen body whose naked feet and ankles project stiffly from beneath the coverlet, yet one that lacks neither grace nor dignity. In her remarkable study of the picture, Pamela Askew concludes, "In the last analysis, pictorially, the experience for the apostles, and for all the observers of his scene, is death as illumination."

For unknown reasons the Carmelites rejected this glorious painting. Baglione says it was because of the Virgin's legs being "swollen and bare." Bellori, who had not seen the picture, thought it was because he had painted the swollen body of a dead woman much too realistically. Mancini has a far more exciting explanation; Caravaggio had used as a model for the Virgin "some dirty whore from the Ortaccio," a red-light district in the Campo Marzio. He suspected that the artist's subsequent misfortunes were divine retribution for such a blasphemy. A later legend even claimed that the model was the body of a drowned prostitute, dredged out of the Tiber.

Laerzio Cherubini kept the rejected *Death of the Virgin* for some years. Early in 1607 it was bought by Vincenzo Gonzaga, Duke of Mantua, on the advice of Peter Paul Rubens, who had seen it in Rome and reported that it was unquestionably one of Caravaggio's finest works. Before it left Rome for the fabulous Gonzaga collection at Mantua, it was exhibited for a week and warmly admired by many of the city's artists. Later, it was bought by King Charles I of England.

On 7 February 1602, Caravaggio signed a contract for another altarpiece, *The Inspiration of St. Matthew*, which would show the saint in the process of writing his Gospel. It was commissioned for the Contarelli Chapel by the Abbate Giacomo Crescenzi, who agreed to pay him 150 scudi. When he had finished, sometime during 1602, it was placed over the chapel's altar. However, Bellori informs us, "it was taken down by the priests, who said that the figure had neither a saint's dignity nor semblance, sitting with crossed legs and feet rudely exposed to the people."

"Caravaggio was in despair," writes Bellori. Already, he must have been despondent enough over the *Death of the Virgin*'s rejection. Fortunately, "the Marchese Vincenzo Giustiniani intervened on his behalf and helped him find a way out of this unpleasant situation; after negotiating with the priests, he bought the painting for himself while persuading him to paint another, which is still to be seen over the altar." The new version, often known as *St. Matthew and the Angel,* amused Berenson by "the incongruity of the stately elder with one knee on a wooden stool, as if he had jumped out of bed to dash off a happy thought or phrase before it escaped him." Even so, it is a magnificent image of divine inspiration.

In 1602, while working on the *Inspiration*, Caravaggio had signed a contract to paint an *Entombment of Christ* for the Vittrici family chapel in the

Oratorian church of Santa Maria in Vallicella. In Caravaggio's day the building remained just as Filippo Neri had wanted it, plain, with whitewashed walls, which made the *Entombment* even more impressive for contemporaries. This time the Virgin was portrayed as a dignified mother superior in late middle age, wearing a nun's coif, not as an attractive young woman; the artist was taking no chances after all the fuss over the model in the *Death of the Virgin*. Christ's body is being lifted down from the Cross. Since the painting was hung over an altar where Mass was celebrated every day, when the priest said "This is my body" as he elevated the Host, it proclaimed the Catholic doctrine of transubstantiation, attacked with such fury by Protestants. Once again, Caravaggio's carefully thought out composition was doing exactly what the Council of Trent asked, and, as always, his grasp of theology was impeccable. For a man of his time, it was still the most important of the sciences, a matter of eternal life, or eternal death.

He was probably much better educated than we realize. His friends were not uncultivated: two poets, the Cavaliere Marino and Aurelio Orsi; an architect, Onorio Longhi; and an unnamed bookseller. Paintings like *Narcissus* indicate at least a smattering of classical learning, and he seems to have read Baronius's *Roman Martyrology*.

At some time during the second half of 1603, he painted *The Sacrifice of Abraham* for Monsignor—soon to be Cardinal—Maffei Barberini. In this alarmingly violent picture, now at the Uffizi, a tough young angel is telling Abraham to spare his shrieking son as he raises his knife to cut the boy's throat. What was so revolutionary was to show Abraham as savagely cruel and Isaac as struggling desperately, instead of piously submissive. It has been argued recently that, in what is very far from being a naturalistic rendering of the story of the sacrifice, Abraham symbolizes God's wrath and Isaac mankind atoning for the sin of Adam, while the angel is Christ interceding, and Abraham's obedience to God is meant to stress the Catholic doctrine of justification by works.

Caravaggio also painted Monsignor Barberini's portrait, now in a private collection at Florence. He depicts a suave, cultivated senior bureaucrat, one of the handful of men who governed Rome and Roman Catholicism. In 1623 Barberini would be elected pope, taking the name "Urban VIII." Del Monte may have introduced the artist to the Monsignor, who was a member of the Accademia degli Insensati.

Most of Caravaggio's many other portraits have been lost, although some may await discovery. Among them were those of his friend Onorio Longhi, Onorio's wife, Caterina, and members of the Crescenzi family. One especially interesting sitter was the Cavaliere Marino, who had been generally acknowledged, since Tasso's death, as Italy's greatest living poet. Marino's praise for the Medusa shield prompted del Monte to give it to Grand Duke Ferdinand, while he introduced Caravaggio to the Crescenzi. Another sitter was Cardinal Benedetto Giustiniani.

During the 1990s a small portrait at the Uffizi of the Vatican librarian, Cardinal Baronius, has sometimes been attributed to Caravaggio, but that has not received general acceptance. If he really did paint Baronius, it would certainly confirm the impression that his sitters were beginning to include an imposing selection of the most influential men in Counter-Reformation Rome. The greatest church historian of his day, a man who had been one of Filippo Neri's first followers, the Oratorian Baronius was Pope Clement's confessor, spiritual adviser, and closest friend.

Caravaggio's friendship with the two Giustiniani brothers continued to flourish. For Vincenzo, he painted an *Amor Vincit Omnia,* a laughing Cupid. The German artist Joachim von Sandrart, who long after Caravaggio was dead spent ten industrious years at the Palazzo Giustiniani recording the marchese's cherished collection in drawings, recounts how "this picture was displayed in a room together with a hundred and twenty others by famous artists, but at my suggestion it was covered with a dark green curtain and only shown when the others had been seen, because it made all the rest seem inferior." Post-Freudian critics have tended to exaggerate the Cupid's homoerotic quality.

By now, Caravaggio had become an almost exclusively religious painter, with very little time for secular subjects. Whether by accident or design, he had made himself the Counter-Reformation's foremost champion on canvas. Even so, if one is to judge from his private life, he was a most unlikely apostle of orthodoxy.

XVII

The Swordsman, 1600–1606

In Flanders, Carel van Mander heard strange rumors about Caravaggio from friends in Rome. In 1603 he wrote that Caravaggio was doing "wonderful things," having risen from obscurity by sheer ability, determination, and hard work, but "after working for a week or two, he wanders round for as long as two months on end, with his rapier by his side and followed by his servant, strolling from one tennis court to another, always ready to fight a duel or start a brawl, so that it is seldom very comfortable to be in his company."

A recent book, *Caravaggio assassino* (1994), claims that he had close links with one of the sinister robber gangs that terrorized Rome by night, but this is untrue. He was not a criminal, merely unbalanced. During a court case in 1603 he referred to "Mario, a painter," who can only have been Mario Minniti. "This Mario once lived with me, but left three years ago, and I haven't spoken to him since." According to Minniti's earliest biographer, he left because he could not put up with Caravaggio's "disorderliness." Later, after marrying, he fled from Rome, apparently after killing a man in a duel.

Earning the income of a minor, well-to-do nobleman or a prosperous merchant, Caravaggio could do as he pleased. Restraints on his private life may have had something to do with his leaving del Monte's household; the cardinal had begun to think that he had "a most strange brain." In September 1603 he moved out of the Palazzo Maffei, taking rooms in the Campo Marzio, in a house in the Vicolo San Biagio. His landlady was a highly respectable widow. While he had no wish to live in the cramped quarters provided by del Monte, he was anxious to stay near him, in case of trouble with the police.

Baglione, who knew Caravaggio personally and disliked him intensely, tells us that "because of an excessively fearless temperament, he sometimes went looking for a chance to break his neck, or to put somebody else's in danger." Yet even Baglione had to admit that he was only "a little," not wholly, dissolute. Bellori says that painting could not calm Caravaggio, that after working for a few hours he would stroll around Rome, pretending to be a soldier. He wore "the costliest silks and velvets like a nobleman, but once he had put on a suit, he left it on until it was in rags." Often he slept in his clothes and always he wore his dagger in bed. He was careless about washing, and for many years used an old portrait as a tablecloth.

All the early sources agree that he was an exceptionally difficult man. Baglione found him "sarcastic and haughty," but what really annoyed him was a withering contempt for all Mannerists, dead or alive, including Baglione. "He spoke ill of all the painters of the past, and of the present day too, however distinguished they might be; because he was convinced that he had surpassed everyone else in the profession." Sandrart says, "It was not easy to get on with him."

But Caravaggio was not invariably disagreeable. He could be surprisingly fair-minded; on at least one occasion he described Arpino, whom he loathed, as a good painter. Although disreputable, his boon companions, if Sandrart can be believed, were cheerful enough, "young men, most of them stout fellows, painters and swordsmen." His close friends stayed loyal to him. Onorio Longhi, a Lombard like himself, fought at his side in at least one duel, while Mario Minniti was delighted to meet him again in Sicily many years later, and long after his death the Cavaliere Marino wrote an affectionate poem in his memory. His patrons went out of their way to protect him, and it is unlikely that they valued him for his art alone. Nevertheless, his signs of a profoundly unhappy nature are unmistakable.

The first suggestion of a disorderly private life came in May 1598, when the *sbirri* caught him wearing a rapier without a permit. He told the police magistrate, "Yesterday, I was arrested at about two o'clock at night between Piazza Madama and Piazza Navona because I was wearing a sword, which I wear as painter to Cardinal del Monte, since I'm one of the cardinal's men and in his service and lodge in his house, and my name is written down on the list of his household."

The next hint of rowdiness was in October 1600, when Onorio Longhi was charged with insulting and attacking Marco Tullio, a painter. During his defense, Longhi said his friend Caravaggio had intervened between Tullio and himself, pulling them apart. At no time had "Michele" drawn his sword, as alleged; recovering from an illness and barely able to stand, he was so weak that a servant had to carry it for him. "Marco Tullio grabbed his scabbard and threw it at me," claimed Longhi. The story of Caravaggio's illness does not sound very convincing, as it was far from unusual for a servant to carry his master's sword.

In November of the same year, Caravaggio was accused of assault by a Tuscan, Girolamo Stampa, who alleged that without provocation Caravaggio had dealt him several fierce blows with his fist and the flat of his sword. In February 1601, Caravaggio paid Flavio Canonico, former sergeant of the guard at Castel Sant' Angelo, to settle out of court an action for armed assault, which can only mean that Caravaggio had attacked him with his rapier.

The Baglione libel case opened on 28 August 1603, offering a unique glimpse into the world of Caravaggio, who was arrested and incarcerated in the Tordinona. Giovane Baglione, a moderately talented Roman painter, had been employed on the frescoes at the Vatican and the Lateran. Caravaggio's work so impressed him that he tried to imitate the *Ecstasy of St. Francis.* He then painted a *Divine Love* for Cardinal Giustiniani in an attempt to compete with the *Amor Vincit Omnia*, the laughing Cupid. Although the cardinal did not think Baglione's picture was as good, he was so pleased with it that he rewarded him with a gold chain. The last straw was when he succeeded in obtaining an important commission Caravaggio wanted for a painting at the church of the Gesù. Baglione had, in his own words, painted "a picture of Our Lord's Resurrection for the Father General of the Society of Jesus. Since the unveiling of the picture on Easter Sunday this year, Onorio Longhi, Michelangelo Merisi [da Caravaggio] and Orazio Gentileschi, who had hoped to paint it themselves . . . have been trying to ruin my reputation by speaking ill of me and finding fault with my painting."

The model for Baglione's *Resurrection* has survived, fussy, overcrowded, melodramatic. One can only sigh for the picture Caravaggio might have painted. It has been suggested that the "Black Pope," the Jesuit General, Claudio Acquaviva, did not give Caravaggio the commission because he was afraid he would produce too startling an interpretation of Christ rising from the dead, somewhere between the sacred and profane.

The court was told how verses vilifying Baglione and his art were circulating, supposedly distributed by Caravaggio's servant. Caravaggio said that he knew nothing about the verses, but did not deny describing Baglione's *Resurrection* as "clumsy," or saying "I consider it the worst he's ever done." He added, "I don't know of any artist who thinks that Baglione is a good painter." During the trial Caravaggio defined a good painter as one who could "imitate natural things well." "I believe I know every painter in Rome," he declared, and went on to say that the only ones who were not among his friends were Arpino, Baglione, Gentileschi, and Georg Hoefnagel, "because they don't speak to me—all the rest talk to me and have discussions." The painters he thought really worthwhile (*valentuomini*) were Arpino, Federico Zuccari, Cristofero Roncalli, Annibale Carracci, and Antonio Tempesta. This public tribute to so many of his rivals by Caravaggio refutes Baglione's claim that he despised all painters other than himself.

A crony of Baglione, Mao (Tommaso) Salini, apparently a painter of still lifes, alleged at one hearing that a certain "Giovan Battista" was the *bardassa* of both Caravaggio and Longhi. The word means either a ne'er-do-well or a male prostitute. Clearly, Salini was trying to harm Caravaggio's reputation by implying that he employed young criminals or had homosexual tastes. In response, Caravaggio said that he had never even heard of Giovan Battista, and the court ignored the allegation.

The trial ended inconclusively with Caravaggio being released from the Tordinona on 25 September, after the intervention of the French ambassador, Philippe de Béthune, Comte de Selles. A Florentine Knight of Malta, the Commander Fra' Ainolfo Bardi, gave a guarantee in writing to the governor of Rome, Monsignor Ferrante Taverna, that Caravaggio would do nothing to harm or insult either Baglione or Mao Salini. Even so, he was confined to his house for a time, under pain of being "sent to the galleys" if he left it without permission. It looks very much as though Béthune and Bardi each acted at the prompting of Cardinal del Monte, who did not care to see his favorite artist in prison and unable to paint. The king of France's queen was a sister of the Grand Duke Ferdinand, so in consequence there were close links between France and Tuscany. Since del Monte was Tuscany's representative at Rome, and one of the "French party" among the cardinals, both Béthune and Bardi must have been only too willing to oblige him.

Caravaggio was placed under virtual house arrest because the authorities were desperately anxious to discourage quarrels, which might otherwise end in duels and potentially fatal bloodshed. In November, Onorio Longhi was arrested, Baglione having complained that Longhi was insulting himself and Salini. But on this occasion Caravaggio kept his head down and was left in peace.

Baglione lived for another forty years, becoming president of the Accademia di San Luca and publishing two important books—an account of the new churches that had been built at Rome and a history of Roman artists in recent times. He took a long-delayed revenge on Caravaggio in acknowledging the beauty of his old enemy's paintings, while enlarging on his failings as a human being. Nowhere, in either work, does Baglione make any mention of his quarrel with him.

Meanwhile, the feud between Caravaggio and his old master Arpino simmered on. In 1600, delighted by the frescoes that Arpino had painted at San Giovanni Laterano, Pope Clement had made him a Knight of the Order of Christ, since when he had been styled the "Cavaliere d'Arpino." It was a rare honor for a painter, and it appears to have made Caravaggio fiercely jealous. Joachim von Sandrart recounts how, when Caravaggio met the Cavaliere riding proudly to court, he challenged him to a duel. "Now's the time for us to settle our quarrel, since we're both armed," he shouted, telling him to get down off his horse. The haughty Arpino replied that, as a Papal Knight, he could not possibly fight someone of inferior rank. "So courteous an answer wounded Caravaggio more deeply than any sword thrust," writes Sandrart, who believed it was this exchange that first made him think of becoming a Knight of Malta, to put himself on the same level as Arpino.

He managed to keep out of trouble for several months after the Baglione case, if only because he could not leave his house without permission or was away from Rome on business. Then, in April 1604, a waiter at the Albergo del Moro complained that Caravaggio had thrown a plate of hot artichokes into his face, endangering his eyes, and had threatened to draw his sword; he seems to have escaped with a fine. In October, walking home from dinner at the Torretta with two friends, a bookseller and a member of Cardinal Aldobrandini's household, Caravaggio was arrested on a charge of throwing stones. His reaction was to ask the bookseller to tell del Monte he was back in jail. The arrest took place near the house of a certain "Menicuccia," whose name sounds like a courtesan's. (He has been romantically linked by historians with Menicuccia, unconvincingly identified as the Siennese prostitute

Domenica Calvi.) In November, after insulting a *sbirro* who had demanded to see his license to carry weapons, he spent another spell in the Tordinona.

The *sbirri* must have known "Michelangelo" (or "Michele") only too well by now. The famous painter in his splendid if rumpled clothes had become one of the sights of Rome. Besides the blond servant carrying his rapier, he was always accompanied by a shaggy black dog with the alchemical name of "Cornacchia" ("Raven"), a performer of spectacular tricks.

Unhappily, he kept on being arrested. In May 1605, caught with unlicensed weapons in the small hours of the morning, he went back to the Tordinona. In July, having grossly insulted a woman called Laura, he suffered a further spell in prison. He was bound over not to molest her or her daughter Isabella with verbal abuse or by singing scurrilous verses about them that had been set to music.

At about this time, he tried to fight a duel with Guido Reni, who had replaced him as Cardinal Aldobrandini's choice to paint another *Crucifixion of St. Peter* for the basilica of St. Peter's. Enraged, he accused Guido of "stealing his style and his color." The duel never took place, though Guido was certainly copying his style. Caravaggio later became furiously jealous of the Florentine Passignano (Domenico Cresti), whom he sometimes encountered in taverns. When Passignano was working on yet another *Crucifixion of St. Peter* for the basilica, Caravaggio destroyed his work tent in St. Peter's, cutting it in pieces and shouting at everyone that Passignano's picture was "terrible."

Sometimes, however, he went out drinking at taverns with Passignano's great friend Ludovico Cardi, known as "Il Cigoli" after the castle where he had been born in Tuscany. A painter himself, Il Cigoli seems to have been terrified of upsetting Caravaggio, afraid of provoking his "persecutions and very strange temper."

In July 1605 Caravaggio quarreled over a girl with Mariano Pasqualone, a notary from Accumoli. A few days afterward, he attacked Pasqualone from behind as he was walking past the Spanish ambassador's palace in the Piazza Navona, giving him a sword cut or a blow from a pistol butt on the back of his head. He then ran off and took refuge in the nearby Palazzo Madama. The police report described the girl as "Lena, who stands in Piazza Navona . . . who is Michelangelo's girl." It sounds as though she was a prostitute and Caravaggio was passionately in love with her. From the evidence of his paintings we know that he had acquired a beautiful new model. Professional female models were always prostitutes, and one historian believes Caravaggio attacked Pasqualone because "the notary had had commerce with her." Another thinks she may have been Pasqualone's former fiancée. It is likely, however, that she was Maddalena Antonietti, one of a family of dedicated Roman whores. She and her sister Amabilia were much in demand, their clients including a nephew of the late Pope Sixtus V and the chief of police.

Caravaggio was frightened after attacking Pasqualone that the assault could be interpreted as attempted murder. If he was found guilty, it would mean the gallows. Early in August, he fled to Genoa, but he was back in Rome before the end of the month. Pasqualone settled out of court, no doubt in return for generous compensation. One wonders if del Monte's famous comment on Caravaggio was provoked by the Pasqualone affair. In a letter of August 24, the cardinal was reliably reported as describing him as *uno cervello stravagantissimo*—"a wild, wild, spirit."

In September, Caravaggio's former landlady, Prudenzia Bruni, complained to the authorities that he had thrown stones at her windows and broken her venetian blind. He had not been back to the rooms he rented in her house since his flight to Genoa, so, as he owed her six months' rent, she had obtained a warrant to seize the belongings he had left behind. She told the police she was convinced that he stoned her house in reprisal, "in order to upset me."

In October, the *sbirri* found him lying in the street with sword or dagger wounds in his throat and left ear. They took him to a friend's house nearby, where he recovered. It was obvious that he had been fighting, but he insisted stubbornly that he had merely fallen on his sword. The authorities fined him five hundred scudi, once more placing him under house arrest.

Between 1598 and the end of 1605, he was brought before the magistrates not less than eleven times. Perhaps social ambition, the desire to behave as well as dress like a nobleman, had something to do with his behavior; looking for a fight, especially with the *sbirri*, was a fashionable amusement among the younger Roman nobles, who also enjoyed swaggering round the city pretending to be soldiers. Later, a desire to rise in the world socially was one of Caravaggio's motives for wanting to become a Knight of Malta. Another possible reason for his belligerence is a weakness for the bottle; most of the incidents seem to have taken place after he had dined at a tavern. Even so, neither social climbing nor drunkenness can have been altogether responsible for his relentless brawling. All too clearly, the long history of repeated violence indicates grave inner disturbance. The mood swings hint at some form of depressive illness. Sandrart, another early writer, records how he and his cronies had chosen for their motto *Nec spes, nec metu*—"with neither hope nor fear"—a very peculiar motto for someone so passionate and emotional in his art. To a certain degree, the tension may have been soothed by painting, which would partly explain his prolific output and why he nearly always delivered on time.

It is particularly unfortunate that there should have been so many frustrations in his professional life. Again and again he failed to obtain a commission for St. Peter's, at that time the topmost pinnacle of every Italian artist's ambition. Most unfairly, each of the cardinals who ran the *Fabbrica di San Pietro* preferred to choose a painter who came from his own part of Italy, instead of allotting the commissions according to talent. As time went by, Caravaggio became understandably infuriated that a succession of mediocre rivals should be rewarded, while he was invariably passed over. He was very conscious of his own genius, yet professional disappointment, however intense, cannot account for the baffling contrast between the spirituality of Caravaggio's art and his squalid police record.

XVIII

"Wonderful Things at Rome," 1603

When Carel van Mander wrote of Caravaggio's disreputable private life, he added that he was "doing wonderful things at Rome." "He will not make a single brush stroke without a close study from life, which he copies and paints." Undoubtedly, Caravaggio produced some of his finest work during this later Roman period. In January 1604, he went to Tolentino, not far from the Adriatic coast, where he had been invited to paint an altarpiece for the Capuchin church of the Crocefisso. No trace of such a picture survives. But having made the long journey from Rome to Tolentino it seems unlikely that he would have omitted to make a pilgrimage to Loreto, the Counter-Reformation Lourdes, which was only a few miles away.

According to a widely believed tradition, during the thirteenth century, the house in Nazareth where the Blessed Virgin was born, and where Jesus spent his childhood, was carried away by angels through the sky, first to Dalmatia and then to Loreto. It was a tiny brick building, twenty-eight feet by twelve, and thirteen feet high. Countless pilgrims flocked to it in the hope of finding miraculous cures, or to pray for divine intervention. It was a place of last resort, when everything else had failed. It was also a place where sinners were sent by their confessors, to atone for their misdeeds.

Quivering with horror at the "shamefull opinions of the Papists" and their "idolatry," the daring Scots tourist William Lithgow came here in 1609, only six years after Caravaggio. As a Calvinist, he observed scornfully that when any of his Catholic companions approached the town gate, they pulled off their shoes and stockings, walking barefoot to the shrine, "many hundreds of bare-footed, blinded bodies, creeping on their hands and knees." He also learned that every year these pilgrims offered "many rich gifts, amounting to an unspeakable value, as Chaines, & Rings of Gold and Silver, Rubies, Diamonds, Silken Tapestries, Goblets, imbrouderies, and such like."

In Loreto's narrow streets Caravaggio saw the crippled and the palsied, the blind and the deaf, the fevered and the crazed. Courtiers came because the shrine had the power to render poison harmless; military men because it could deflect bullets or sword cuts; barren women because it could overcome infertility. Rich and poor, they prayed before the Holy House, which stood inside a church with a dome by Sangallo and side chapels by Bramante.

The shrine had already cast its spell over another painter, Lorenzo Lotto, who had died there as a lay brother in 1557, and who may have influenced Caravaggio. There are paintings by him in the Apostolic Palace that must have been in the church in 1603. If Caravaggio came to Loreto on a pilgrimage, perhaps as a penitent, he is likely to have done so on the feast of the Nativity in September, or of the Translation (removal) of the Holy House in December. Apparently the simplest, humblest pilgrims made the most impression on him.

Entering the church through bronze doors, Caravaggio found its walls covered by frescoes and paintings that told the story of Loreto. Seven massive silver lamps burned before the Santa Casa. Inside, there was an ancient, wonder-working Madonna and Child, carved from wood and black with age, dressed in silks and velvets, ablaze with jewels. Sometimes the statue seemed to come alive, electrifying the pilgrims.

When Caravaggio returned to Rome, he was able to pay special tribute to the Santa Casa. A certain Ermete Cavalleti had bequeathed five hundred scudi to adorn a chapel with a picture of the Virgin of Loreto, and for this purpose his heirs had purchased the first side chapel on the left in the church of Sant' Agostino. Probably during the latter half of 1603 they commissioned Caravaggio to paint a *Madonna di Loreto*. The altarpiece that resulted could have been painted only by someone who had felt the full impact of the Holy House, and who understood what it meant to the pilgrims.

In this extremely moving picture, sometimes called the *Madonna dei Pellegrini*, Caravaggio shows the "standing Madonna holding the child in her arms in the act of blessing; kneeling in front are two pilgrims with hands folded in prayer, a poor man with bare feet and legs, with a leather cap and a staff resting on his shoulder, who is accompanied by an old woman with a cap on her head," Bellori writes. Few modern observers appreciate that the couple's feet are bare out of piety, not from poverty. A strikingly beautiful model with a very strong face posed for the Virgin. She was almost certainly Lena.

Baglione sneers that one of the pilgrims has muddy feet, while the other wears a dirty, torn cap. But in trying to belittle the painting, he testifies to its popularity, reporting disdainfully how "the common people [*popolani*] made a great fuss [*estremo schiamazzo*] about it." The picture was every simple pilgrim's idea of Loreto, of the Virgin appearing miraculously with the child Jesus at the door of the Santa Casa, welcoming those who came in humble simplicity. This was the art envisaged by the Council of Trent.

In fairness to Baglione, many educated people must have agreed with him. Nowadays, it is difficult for us to grasp just how much Caravaggio's preference for ugly, shabby, lower-class humanity as models shocked contemporaries. Until Victorian times, artists generally depicted men and women as handsome, well groomed, and upper-class when painting scenes from Scripture or history. An Oratorian might have approved, but not many others, apart from common, illiterate folk.

In 1605 Cesare d'Este, duke of Modena, commissioned a Madonna from Caravaggio as an altarpiece for a church at his capital. For once, the artist was late in finishing, or at least in delivering it. Cesare wrote to Cardinal del Monte, asking him to help. Del Monte warned the duke not to be too hopeful, adding that Caravaggio had recently declined six thousand scudi from Prince Doria to paint a fresco. Some years later, Caravaggio sold a *Madonna of the Rosary,* which may have begun as the picture ordered by the duke of Modena.

Another altarpiece from about this time was the *Madonna dei Palafrenieri,* the Virgin and Child with a stern St. Anne (the Virgin's mother). He used the same model for the Virgin as in the *Madonna di Loreto.* The figures are stamping on the head of a hissing serpent, which may be intended as an emblem of Protestantism. Ordered for the chapel of the Papal Grooms (*Palafrenieri*) at St. Peter's, it was just the sort of commission Caravaggio had been seeking. But although he was paid the stipulated price of seventy-five scudi, much less than his normal fee, in Baglione's smug words "it was removed by command of the Lords Cardinal of the Fabbrica [di San Pietro]." The rejection must have made Caravaggio more bitter than ever and perhaps accounts for some of his violent misbehavior.

He painted a *St. John the Baptist* for the Genoese banker Ottavio Costa, who gave a copy as an altarpiece for the church of a Ligurian village where he was feudal lord. It may have been painted during the artist's very brief exile at Genoa in 1605, when he fled there after attacking the notary Pasqualone. If his mind was troubled, he worked with greater speed than ever. A banker in Rome, Costa, one of his warmest admirers, came from the gentry of the town of Albenga in Liguria. He was the first owner of *Judith and Holofernes,* eventually possessing five Caravaggios and leaving a clause in his will that his heirs were to sell none of them.

Caravaggio continued to paint other pictures besides altarpieces, but these, too, were invariably religious. In a *Crowning with Thorns,* commissioned by Vincenzo Giustiniani, a pair of sadistic executioners are forcing thorns into Christ's head, his blood pouring down, while an armored centurion looks on with perverted pleasure. An *Ecce Homo,* Christ presented to the Jews by Pilate, was painted in response to a request from a Monsignor Massimi. The patient Christ is almost excessively gentle and resigned. In contrast, Pontius Pilate is much more interesting. Ludicrously respectable and fussily bad-tempered, he could easily have been modeled on one of the detested police magistrates with whom Caravaggio had so often come in contact so unpleasantly. What he had not been told was that Monsignor Massimi had slyly commissioned several versions of the subject in a concealed competition between three artists, without telling any of them that they were competing. The version by Il Cigolo pleased the Monsignor best. It was another unfair and humiliating rejection.

There is unmistakable pain on the faces in many of the paintings from Caravaggio's later years in Rome. Costa's *St. John the Baptist* wears a sulky, even lowering look. Disturbance is still more apparent in two somber studies of Francis of Assisi that date from this time. They show not the slightest suggestion of ecstasy. But, although they are not self-portraits, both portray someone of the same physical type as Caravaggio—small, black-bearded, unkempt. There could be no more eloquent expression of Caravaggio's very personal and strange blend of the most sincere spirituality with the most profound unhappiness than these two paintings of St. Francis.

XIX

The First Baroque Pope, 1605

Clement VIII died in March 1605, and by the end of spring Paul V was pontiff. Clement is often described as the last of the Counter-Reformation popes, while Paul is sometimes called the first "Baroque" pope. This is an oversimplification. The Counter-Reformation remained very much alive even if the Baroque was in full swing by the end of Paul's reign.

Despite Clement's indecisiveness, he had been surprisingly successful, and not merely because of his saintly life and austere court. He had restored the Papacy's political influence to an extent that had not been seen for centuries. France was saved for Catholicism, while both the French and the Spanish competed for Rome's favor.

Inevitably, a papal conclave to choose a new pope was fraught with tension. So, too, was the entire city of Rome. Everyone knew that a completely new court with new favorites was about to emerge. From the moment the Cardinal Camerlengo took the Fisherman's ring from the dead pontiff's hand, he ruled Rome in his place until the election of a new pope, and struck coins that bore his own name. In practice, during a conclave the city was virtually ungoverned. Armed guards were doubled outside the palaces, with chains placed across their gateways. A "Lantern edict," ordering householders to place a light at a window each night, did little to deter wrongdoers. The *sbirri* were far too busy to worry about the brawls of Caravaggio and his friends.

The cardinals were divided into French and Spanish factions, and there was much lobbying. News of the surprisingly swift election on April 1 of the elderly Alessandro de' Medici was greeted in Paris by fireworks and cannon fire. But the new pope, Leo XI, died before the end of the month, so the conclave reassembled. On May 16 it chose the mild-mannered, gentle-seeming Cardinal Borghese.

Like more than a few pontiffs, Camillo Borghese's mild manners and gentleness soon vanished. In Ranke's words, "immediately after his election, Paul V evinced a peculiarly rugged disposition." From then on, Rome was to be ruled by an iron and seemingly merciless hand. A penniless, half-insane Lombard scholar had written a ridiculous parallel history of Clement VIII and Tiberius Caesar, comparing the late pope to the sinister Roman emperor. The manuscript stayed in his garret until he foolishly showed it to a woman in the same house, who denounced him. He was arrested with all Rome laughing at the story. There was a general impression that Pope Paul would take a lenient view, several people petitioning him to show mercy, but the wretched man was beheaded on the Ponte Sant' Angelo, and his pitiful possessions were confiscated. Paul swiftly issued draconian edicts against loose women, swindling innkeepers, and those who spread false news. Gentlemen faced still sterner penalties for wearing swords. Although the edicts were largely ignored or evaded, everyone in Rome was uncomfortably aware of an unusually frightening presence on the papal throne.

Some historians believe that Caravaggio's prospects were darkened by Paul's election; in reality they had never looked brighter, and if the pope, the future patron of Bernini, was more interested in architecture and sculpture than in painting, his nephew was a very different story. By the end of Paul's reign, Cardinal Scipione Borghese had amassed one of the most wonderful private collections known to history.

Caravaggio did his best to satisfy so important a customer. "For the same Cardinal, he painted St. Jerome, who is shown writing, absorbed, and reaching out a hand to dip into the inkwell," Bellori tells us. The artist's portrayal of the compiler of the Vulgate derived from the account in *The Golden Legend*: "After doing penance for four years, he went to Bethlehem and obtained permission to dwell at the Lord's crib like an animal." Fasting each day until evening, "he persevered in his holy resolution, and labored for fifty-five years and six months at translating the Scriptures." The picture is still to be seen at the Villa Borghese.

The painting delighted Cardinal Scipione, whose collection eventually included thirteen Caravaggios. Five of them were confiscated from the Cavaliere d'Arpino, no longer the pope's favorite artist, since he fell foul of the authorities over tax arrears. Scipione was a ruthless collector of pictures, imprisoning at least one rash artist who failed to oblige him. He could be equally forceful, however, in defending his favorites, and his benevolent role in Caravaggio's career has been underestimated. He tried to protect him whenever he could, even in exile.

Caravaggio's new patron was not only the cardinal nephew, but the cardinal secretary of state as well, the most powerful person in Rome after his uncle. While the Venetian ambassador may have reported that the cardinal nephew was not particularly clever, he was undeniably astute. As soon as Scipione received the Red Hat, shortly after his maternal uncle's election, he changed his name from Cafarelli to Borghese. He knew how to interpret Pope Paul's wishes and ensure that they were put into effect. Nor could anyone deny his good taste.

We know what Scipione looked like from Bernini's bust, almost comically corpulent and heavy-jowled but nonetheless impressive. He was unusually amiable, famous for his charm and tact. Romans who sampled his sumptuous hospitality called it *delicium orbis*, the world's delight. Although no scandals of the flesh were ever linked to him, his wildly extravagant expenditure on food and drink earned him a rebuke from the pope on at least one occasion. It was common knowledge that within a few years he possessed an income of 140,000 scudi, and eventually he appropriated four percent of the entire papal revenue, enabling him to indulge to the full his passion for the arts. Bellori records in his lives that the Cardinal Scipione Borghese was so pleased with the pictures Caravaggio had painted "that he introduced him to the Pontiff, Paul V, of whom he painted a seated portrait, being richly rewarded by the said lord."

Even Caravaggio must have been cowed by the prospect of painting the pope. No doubt he had to go through the ritual of alternately bowing and genuflecting at his first audience, since Paul was a stickler for protocol. He was a burly man of imposing presence, ponderous and taciturn. Heavily overweight, it was rumored that he sweated to such an extent at night that his barber had to comb his hair for an hour every morning to dry his head.

The authenticity of Caravaggio's portrait of Paul V, which remains at the Villa Borghese, has occasionally been questioned on the grounds that it seems too tame. But faced with an exceptionally formidable sitter, ferociously careful of his dignity, Caravaggio is unlikely to have tried to make his subject adopt a striking pose. An unpleasant look in His Holiness's eyes, verging on the malevolent, has been ascribed to short sight.

The pope's patronage of the arts, and his nephew's, undoubtedly helped to usher in the Baroque Age. No one knows when the term "Baroque" was first used, but the movement was fundamentally religious in inspiration, set in motion by the Counter-Reformation. Despite its exuberance, it was haunted by an all-pervading concentration on death and dying and how to face them. More than a few Baroque artists attended public executions, or watched corpses being dissected. Their age coincided with a long period of peace in Italy, when turbulent natures could find outlets only in the most savage violence.

The Counter-Reformation, which gave birth to the Baroque, succeeded because it harnessed profound human impulses, whether the female principle through the cult of the Madonna or the need for forgiveness through confession. Its gorgeous liturgy satisfied a thirst for theater and color while, despite its leaders' asceticism, it exalted the human body and was not afraid of nudity in art. Baroque had genuine popular appeal. Instead of using classical Antiquity, accessible to only a small, highly educated audience, as had Renaissance art, it concentrated on the religion of the humble as well as that of the elite. Its novelties were breathtaking, and a novelty like Caravaggio's experiments with light—compared by Kenneth Clark to the kind of lighting fashionable in films of the 1920s—had enormous dramatic impact. So long as the Catholic revival continued, Baroque art would retain its vitality.

Most of us have colorful images of the Baroque churches in their full, triumphant splendor, with gilded altars crowned by sunbeams amid serpentine columns, walls of marble, porphyry, and scagliola, even of bronze and silver, and statues of swooning saints. All this was still in the process of emerging when Caravaggio died. Because of his uncompromising realism and avoidance of decoration, many historians do not see him as an artist belonging to the Baroque. "Baroque is the last epithet I would apply to Caravaggio, although it is the one he is now so often graced with," grumbled Berenson. "Indeed, a more descriptive one would be the un-Baroque, or even the anti-Baroque."

Nevertheless, the churches for which Caravaggio painted his altarpieces, his greatest achievements, are unmistakably Baroque. And he was very much aware of these churches, painting his altarpieces in such a way that, if they have been removed to a gallery, they must be viewed from six feet below if they are to be appreciated properly. For all his realism, he cannot be understood outside a Baroque context. Certainly, no one can question that Caravaggio belonged to the Counter-Reformation. His utterly sincere, down-to-earth treatment of sacred subjects moved the faithful deeply, and no artist was more successful in proclaiming the new Catholicism. As the first anniversary of Paul V's accession drew near, Caravaggio's prospects must have seemed enviable. His work was admired and collected by the all-powerful cardinal secretary, whose favorite he had become, and he had painted the pope himself.

XX

The Killing of Ranuccio Tommasoni, May 1606

If you listen to the ringing martial music of Monteverdi's *Combat Between Tancredi and Clorinda,* you may catch a faint echo of the secret approval Caravaggio's contemporaries felt for men who fought duels. It is not surprising that Monteverdi found inspiration for his warlike "dramatic dialogue" in a battle scene from the *Gerusalemme Liberata* for, although Tasso was the reverse of a duelist, he was famous for realistic descriptions of single combat. Montaigne, in his essay "Cowardize, the Mother of Crueltie," also recognized Tasso's gift for describing a fight to the death, quoting a stanza in which the poet explained just what it felt like to fence for one's life with a mixture of rage and fear. Every literate man and woman in Rome read Tasso. Even if they admired the duelists, they can have had no illusions about the lethal, often vicious nature of dueling. The Roman authorities had no illusions either. They regarded duels as an unmitigated nuisance, and, if caught, survivors went to the scaffold.

An *avviso* of 31 May 1606, reports the event that ruined Caravaggio's life and very nearly ended it, after his refusal to pay Ranuccio Tommasoni a bet of ten scudi, lost over a game of tennis. Until recently, all we knew about Tommasoni was that he came from Terni and was "a young man with very good manners" in Baglione's opinion. Caravaggio sounded like a savage bully picking a fight with a callow teenager. But from recently discovered evidence, the reverse was true. Ranuccio, who called himself "Captain Tommasoni," was a swaggering thug whose brother, Giovan Francesco, was *caporione*, or nominal captain, of the Campo Marzio district (*rione*) and therefore its local gang boss. Giovan Francesco and his two brothers appear to have terrorized the Campo Marzio by night. Only the year before, the three, unlawfully "armed with sword, dagger and pistol," had led the Campo Marzio "guard" against the *sbirri,* disputing the arrest of some criminals who were probably under their protection. In the ensuing brawl, several men had been wounded and at least one killed.

On the evening of Sunday, 29 May, Caravaggio and some friends were passing Tommasoni's house in Via della Scrofa when Tommasoni suddenly emerged with his cronies, challenging him to fight. During the ensuing combat, says the *avviso,* "the painter was wounded and Captain Petronio came to his rescue. Ranuccio's brother, a captain too, was on the other side with several more friends, so that as many as a dozen took part. Finally, Tommasoni lost his balance and fell over, a sword thrust leaving him dead on the ground."

Mancini's version is that "Caravaggio killed his enemy, helped by Onorio Longhi," while Baglione reports that "after Caravaggio had wounded him in the thigh, Ranuccio fell down, and he killed him as he lay on the ground." Bellori, clearly less well informed, states that "during a game of tennis with a young man who was a friend, they began hitting each other with their rackets and then drew their swords, so that he killed the youth, but was himself wounded." Sandrart, still more imaginative, believes the duel had its origins in Caravaggio's quarrel with the Cavaliere d'Arpino.

Another account, only recently discovered and dated 3 June 1606, confirms the story in the *avvisi*, together with the details given by Mancini and Baglione. "Because of some game near the Grand Duke's palace, a quarrel broke out between a son of the late Colonel Lucantonio [Tommasoni] da

Terni and the celebrated painter, Michelangelo da Caravaggio, in which Tommasoni fell dead from a thrust delivered when he had fallen to the ground. His brother Gio. Francesco and Captain Petronio, a Bolognese friend of Caravaggio, joined in the affray, during which the said Gio. Francesco mortally wounded Captain Petronio and Caravaggio in the head, after which he and Caravaggio fled, and Petronio was put in prison, where he remains under guard."

The most plausible reconstruction of what took place is that Caravaggio and Tommasoni both had five seconds. Those on Ranuccio's side included his brothers, Alessandro and Giovan Francesco, the latter being the gang boss of the Campo Marzio, with two unknown friends. On Caravaggio's there were Onorio Longhi, Captain Petronio (otherwise known as "Antonio da Bologna"), and perhaps Aurelio Orsi. (The historian Maurizio Calvesi suggests that Mario Minniti may have been one of the others.) They fought separate combats with each other until they had disabled their opponents, then went to their comrades' aid. After disposing of his own enemy, Longhi rushed to help Caravaggio, knocking Tommasoni's rapier aside with his sword, or throwing a cloak over it, so that Caravaggio was able to bring Tommasoni down and give him a final thrust as he lay prostrate. Having finished with Petronio, Giovan Tommasoni ran up to avenge his brother, giving Caravaggio a thrust in the head. At that point, the *sbirri* appeared, and the combatants left hastily.

Ranuccio Tommasoni appears to have been the only man killed outright in the duel, although Petronio was fatally wounded and Caravaggio badly injured. It is only fair to point out that Caravaggio did not start the fight.

Everyone who had taken part fled from Rome as soon as possible. Prevented from doing so by his wound, Petronio was arrested, although no record has been discovered of his fate; he probably died in prison. Onorio Longhi succeeded in reaching his Lombard homeland, where he was later joined by his wife and children. Despite eloquent pleading that he had not killed anybody and had tried to restrain Caravaggio, Longhi's petition to be allowed to return to Rome was not granted for several years.

It was very different for Caravaggio, who most certainly had killed somebody. Slaying Ranuccio was murder and meant the death penalty. Already well known to the *sbirri,* if caught he would have been immediately brought before a police magistrate, and his head would swiftly have joined those rotting on the Ponte Sant' Angelo. Too badly wounded to escape from Rome at once, he hid in the Palazzo Giustiniani, sheltered by Vincenzo, until he regained enough strength to be able to travel. For the moment, the *sbirri* did not dare break into a palace with such important owners, and clearly the Giustiniani brothers were ready to protect him.

Fortunately, some very influential and powerful people were determined to see that he got away. If his patrons were distressed by his private life, irritated by his difficult temperament, and shocked by the news of the duel, they had no wish to see the end of a man who painted such wonderful pictures. Significantly, Cardinal Borghese bought the *Madonna dei Palafrenieri* less than three weeks after the duel, paying a hundred scudi, although he could easily have confiscated it. Nor is it beyond the bounds of possibility that the cardinal secretary discreetly warned the chief of police that he would not be overjoyed if the *sbirri* succeeded in making an arrest in this particular case. Apparently it was the agents of the painter's old friend the Marchesa di Caravaggio who told him where he could find refuge after leaving the city.

He soon recovered his strength, escaping from Rome on the Wednesday after the duel. He dared not go back to his lodgings to collect money for his flight, so obviously someone supplied him with funds. Eluding the *sbirri,* he managed to get away safely; like William Lithgow, dodging the Inquisition three years later, he may have "leapt the walles of Rome" at midnight, since the guards at the gates would have been looking out for him. Bellori says he was followed, but, if he was, he quickly threw his pursuers off his trail. Then he disappeared.

Among the reasons for such a successful escape was the fact that the *sbirri* did not know where he was making for, or where he was hoping to find shelter. The countryside immediately around Rome was an uninviting choice for a hiding place, the Roman Campagna being plagued by malaria, and in any case they would have been able to track him down there through their contacts with the *banditti*. Their first reaction was to expect that, as a Lombard, he would head north. On 31 May, the day of his escape, the Modenese agent at Rome reported rumors that Caravaggio had fled "in the direction of Florence and may perhaps go to Modena." In reality, he had gone to ground at a much safer haven, only a few miles away.

Five minutes of swordsmanship, probably less, had ended not only in the death of Caravaggio's challenger but in his own ruin. Few turning points in the career of a great artist have been so dramatic. The idol of Rome's younger artists, the favorite of cardinals, the man who had painted the pope's portrait, had suddenly become a hunted murderer with a price on his head.

XXI

Outlaw in the Roman Hills, Summer 1606

Caravaggio spent the summer of 1606 in the hills east of Rome. He was perfectly safe, hidden away in the strongholds of people who could be trusted. But he dared not forget for a moment that he was an outlaw on the run and a bounty would be paid for his head.

There is no record of where he first found shelter after escaping from Rome at the end of May. He seems to have gone north, though not in the direction expected by the *sbirri*. Leaving no trace, he disappeared northeastward into the Sabine Hills, staying in impregnable mountaintop castles, and then, quite soon, moved farther south. Probably, he was never more than thirty miles from Rome. The Marchesa di Caravaggio, or someone close to her, had swiftly found secure refuges for him, in particular at her Colonna kinsmen's hill towns of Palestrina, Zagarolo, and Paliano. It is also likely that some of his patrons—del Monte, the Giustiniani brothers, Ottavio Costa, and perhaps even Scipione Borghese—provided him with money.

Luckily, he had had plenty of opportunity to renew his acquaintance with the Marchesa Costanza. Since the jubilee of 1600, she had often been in Rome, staying with her family at the Palazzo Colonna in the Piazza Santi Apostoli, where he must have visited her. If she was away at the time of the

Tommasoni duel, in Lombardy or at her new palace in Naples, her family could be relied on to help him, fulfilling a feudal obligation to the son of a valued retainer.

Modern roads have brought the Colonna hill towns within a short drive of Rome, but in those days they were dauntingly remote, approached with difficulty along steep mountain paths. During his summer in exile, a forlorn Caravaggio must have ridden from one to another. Naturally, he took very good care to conceal his tracks, so that no record of his itinerary survives. What little we know about his movements has been confused by Mancini and Bellori, who both claim, mistakenly, that he began by hiding at Zagarolo. In reality, his first refuge was probably Palestrina, where his host may have been the new bishop, Cardinal Ascanio Colonna, the marchesa's nephew.

An English tourist, Augustus Hare, visited Palestrina in the 1870s, when it still looked much the same as it had in Caravaggio's day. The huge castle where he stayed was high on a bare hillside where, says Hare, "the sun beats so pitilessly upon its white rocks that it is best to put off the ascent till near sunset." From the summit, Rome and the sea could be seen. Just below the castle was a squalid village, where, according to local legend, St. Peter had lived for a while as a hermit. The town beneath was full of Roman remains, with fragments of classical pillars in every house. It had a minute piazza and a small cathedral. The plain below, Hare recalled, was so rich that it looked like a vast garden of fruit trees. Baglione tells us that Caravaggio painted a *Mary Magdalene* at Palestrina. Only copies survive. They show the Magdalen as penitent and exhausted, rather than ecstatic, no doubt the painter's own frame of mind.

Zagarolo, a mere twenty-one miles from Rome, sounds more comfortable. Only a few years before, the palace had hosted a papal commission working on the text of the Vulgate. Mancini says that here Caravaggio "was secretly entertained by the Prince." This was the marchesa's cousin, Don Marzio Colonna, Duke of Zagarolo. Although a great Roman noble who lived in splendor, he was bankrupt, a victim of inflation. His reputation was slightly sinister. He had had close links with the Cenci; the castle where Count Francesco was murdered belonged to him, while Giacomo Cenci's decision to kill his father may have been prompted by being in debt to the duke. He was also a man of taste, a collector of Antique sculpture. He may be the donor in his guest's *Madonna of the Rosary,* bald, wary-eyed, and commanding. To produce such a likeness, Caravaggio must have met him several times.

Mancini and Bellori state that while Caravaggio was at Zagarolo he painted his second *Christ at Emmaus.* Subtler than the first version, the wise and sensitive Christ is most impressive, while the old woman holding a dish is almost as memorable. Nobody seeing her at the Brera in Milan can deny Caravaggio's compassion for the poor and weak. Mancini believed that the *Supper at Emmaus* was bought by Ottavio Costa, who somehow kept in touch.

It is possible that Caravaggio painted other pictures during his time in the hills. Painting was his only cure for loneliness. Apart from one or two Colonna retainers, the company consisted of peasants, whom Hare described two and a half centuries later as "savage, lawless, violent and avaricious." Ahead lay the dismal prospect of autumn rain and winter snow. He had to move on, and the obvious place to go was Naples.

Even before his flight from Rome, he may have discussed entering the Order of Malta with a senior knight, Fra' Ippolito Malaspina, Prior of Naples. Fra' Ippolito had come to Rome in 1603, to take command of the pope's galleys, and became a prominent figure at the papal court, his dress as a Grand Cross making him an eye-catching figure. Another contact among the Knights was Fra' Ainolfo Bardi, who acted as Caravaggio's surety after the Baglione case. The Giustiniani brothers had a cousin in the Order, Fra' Orazio Giustiniani, while the Marchesa Costanza had a son who was a knight.

More than mere social climbing was involved in Caravaggio's decision to enter the order. Joining meant becoming a monk as well as a knight, and he must have known that he would have to make real sacrifices. It is quite possible he was moved by a desire to atone for his disreputable life, a desire reinforced after the killing of Ranuccio Tomassoni.

His ambition to become a Knight of Malta was apparently his main reason for going to Naples, where he could discuss the idea further and, hopefully, take ship for Malta. He may have heard that Fra' Ippolito was leaving Rome and returning to his priory. He would also be able to find commissions for pictures, ammassing funds to finance his new life in the order.

Reaching Naples would not be easy. The usual route from Rome went along the Via Appia, through the Campagna with its ruined aqueducts and haunted tombs, through the malarial Pontine marshes to Terracina, and from there through Formia, Gaeta, and Capua. But although it was the main road and the most used, it was notoriously unsafe. Fynes Moryson, who went this way in 1594, says that for fear of the *banditti,* no one would risk making the journey alone but rode beside the mail coach, which was always escorted by sixty mounted musketeers. Travelers had to rise before dawn, not daring to go any faster than the coach and the mule train that accompanied it. When an inn came in sight, the musketeers let them gallop ahead and "eat a morsell, or rather devoure it," but as soon as the coach caught up, they had to remount. Captured bandits were beheaded and quartered on the spot; while their heads were sent to Rome to get the bounty, their quarters were hung from trees by the roadside, a sight that added nothing to the gaiety of the journey. More than once, *banditti* managed to overwhelm the musketeers, robbing and killing the travelers.

At the end of September or beginning of October, 1608, Caravaggio left his final refuge in the Roman hills. This was the castle at Paliano, even more inaccessible than Palestrina and Zagarolo, whose walls made it seem still grimmer when seen from far below. The town's feudal lord was the young Don Filippo Colonna, Duke of Paliano, another of the marchesa's nephews. Caravaggio may have traveled to Naples with the mail coach; he could have done so in disguise, joining the coach after it had left Rome. It is more likely, however, that he took some lonely road through the hills, although he would have been in scarcely less danger from *banditti,* who were everywhere. Anxious to be rid of such a well-known fugitive, Don Filippo or his steward may have given him an escort of Colonna men at arms.

Despite managing to avoid the bandits, Caravaggio had every reason to feel apprehensive when he came in sight of the largest and most sinister city in Christendom. Just what sort of a welcome was an outlaw going to receive? Although he had powerful friends in Naples, the Neapolitans might arrest and execute him as a murderer, and claim the money for his head.

XXII

Interlude at Naples, 1606–1607

According to a report from Modena, Caravaggio was still at Paliano on 28 September 1606, supposedly waiting for a pardon. But on 6 October he was paid two hundred ducats at Naples for a new commission. A Roman friend may have reminded him of Pope Paul's sternness toward those who had shed blood, warning that, for the moment, there was no hope of forgiveness. In any case, his plans did not include returning to Rome, while he may have had an invitation from the Marchesa di Caravaggio to come to Naples.

The marchesa had acquired a palace on the Chiaia, on the seafront, presumably to be as near as possible to her second son, Fabrizio Sforza Colonna, a Knight of Malta. Formerly prior of Venice, he had spent four years in prison at Valletta for killing a man in a duel, before being released in 1606 and appointed Captain-General of the Galleys. His mother could scarcely avoid knowing the prior of Naples. Understandably inclined to be sorry for the runaway painter, she could easily have put in a good word for him. Caravaggio may also have heard of the imminent arrival of his old patron, Cardinal del Monte, who came at the end of October, accompanied by a group of Roman nobles, including one of the marchesa's Colonna kinsmen. He stayed until March of the following year and, although there is no evidence, it seems likely that Caravaggio called on the cardinal.

On the great bay beneath Vesuvius, Naples was by turns beautiful and squalid. A population estimated at three hundred thousand, increased daily by migrants, made it three times as big as Rome or Milan. It had hordes of beggars, some so destitute they went about stark naked. The Neapolitans were crammed into an area eight miles square, twelve if the suburbs were included. Their city was a checkerboard of straight, narrow streets laid out on the ancient Greek pattern, with houses six stories tall to make extra space, when at Rome they were seldom as high as three. The people, who looked more Levantine than Italian with their dark skins, were noticeably small. They lived on pasta, which had recently supplanted bread and vegetables as their staple diet. In manner, they were "merry, witty and genial," though the upper classes looked, or tried to look, like Spaniards, affecting a haughty gravity. Everyone spoke a clipped, nasal Italian, very different from Roman or Milanese. To Caravaggio, it must have sounded like a foreign language.

This was the capital of the Two Sicilies, the *Regno*, since the twelfth century the only kingdom in Italy. It had become part of the Spanish empire in 1504, southern Italians accepting Spanish rule largely from fear of being conquered by the Turks. A Spanish viceroy ruled at Naples, attended by a truly regal court. When he processed through the city on foot, a cloth-of-gold canopy was held over his head. Among the disadvantages of a Spanish regime were the troops, not just Spaniards or Walloons but Italians, many of them pardoned *banditti,* underpaid and underfed, who robbed in order to keep alive. The Neapolitans took their revenge, frequently leaving at the crossroads the bodies of soldiers they had stabbed in the back.

The viceroys forced the great nobles to live in the capital, where they built enormous palazzi. "There be in this City very many Pallaces, of Gentlemen, Barons and Princes," noted Fynes Moryson. "Whereupon the City is vulgarly called Napoli Gentile." The great families—Carafa, Caracciolo, Ruffo, Minutolo, Sangro, and the rest—were no less respected than the Massimi or Orsini at Rome. There was an exuberant social life, with lavish balls and masquerades. The Genoese were much in evidence and heartily disliked, the Neapolitans blaming them for the crushing taxation, sometimes attacking them in the streets. Naples should have been very rich, but it was bled white by the duties on such staples as grain and flour.

Yet George Sandys, who saw it in 1611, thought Naples the pleasantest of cities. "Their habit is generally Spanish," he tells us. "The Gentry delighteth much in great horses, whereupon they praunce continually thorow the streets. The number of carossess [coaches] is incredible that are kept in this City, as of the segges [sedan chairs] not unlike to horse-litters, but carried by men. These waite for fares in the corners of streets, as Watermen doe at our wharfes; wherein those that will not foote it in the heate are borne (if they please unseene) about the City." He admired the beauty of the women and their elegant clothes, observing that "silke is a worke-day weare for the wife of the meanest artificer."

Sandys writes of soldiers constantly marching through the streets, so that the Neapolitans' ears were "inured to the sound of drum and fife, as their eyes to the . . . glistering of armours." For Naples, even more than Milan, was a bulwark of Spanish rule in Italy. There was a garrison of four thousand troops, with a further sixteen hundred in the other cities of the Regno, and thirty-seven war galleys.

Caravaggio must have been interested in the courtesans as the main source of models. "The women are generally well featured but excessively libidinous," remarked John Evelyn, who visited Naples in the 1640s. He noted that there were thirty thousand registered prostitutes. One of their tricks during the Carnival was to throw eggshells filled with scented water from their windows, while some were even credited with using witchcraft to ensnare clients. Living mainly in an area near the Porta Capuana, they plied their trade everywhere, not just in the famous Ciriglio tavern, but during Mass at the fashionable churches, by the booths on the Largo del

Youth with a Basket of Fruit

Painted in 1594, when Caravaggio was working
for the Cavaliere d'Arpino, who bought it from him

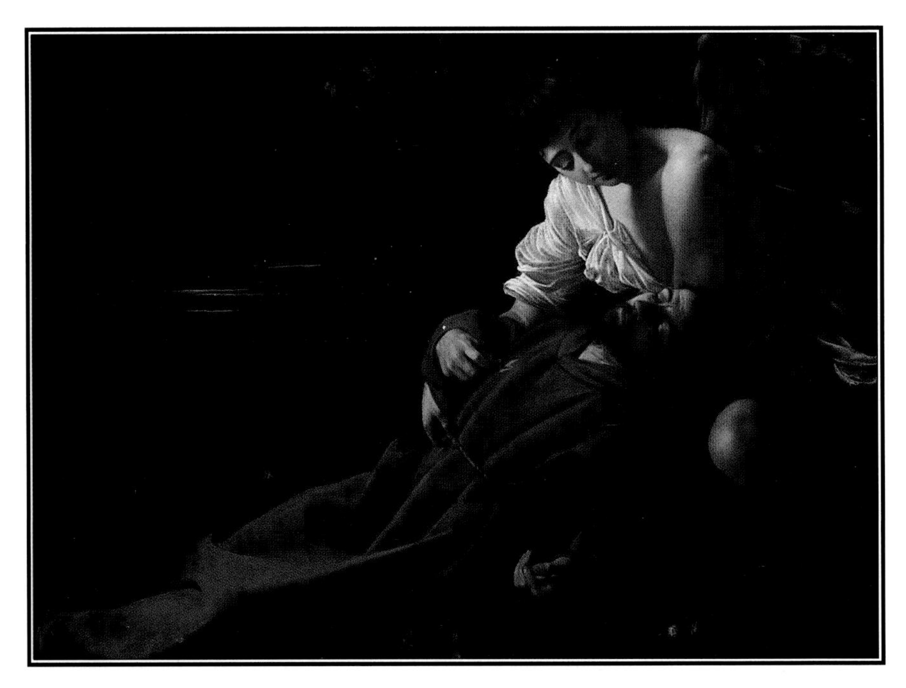

St. Francis in Ecstasy

Painted about 1596, this was the first realistic representation of a mystical ecstasy, so novel that Caravaggio's patron, Cardinal del Monte, feared it would be given a sexual interpretation.

St. Catherine

The model for St. Catherine, painted for Cardinal del Monte in 1598 or 1599, was a famous prostitute, Fillide Melandroni.

Rest on the Flight into Egypt

Caravaggio's most serene painting, this picture from the 1590s may have been painted for Cardinal del Monte.

Judith and Holofernes

Painted toward the end of 1599, and perhaps inspired by the execution of the Cenci that September. Fillide Melandroni was the model for Judith; Holofernes is a self-portrait.

Martyrdom of St. Matthew

Painted in 1599–1600, this is one of the two pictures in the Contarelli Chapel that established Caravaggio's reputation. The bearded King Hyrcanus in the background is a self-portrait.

Basket of Fruit

Owned by del Monte's friend, Cardinal Federigo Borromeo. Caravaggio said that as much patience was needed for a good painting of flowers as for a painting of people.

Conversion of St. Paul

In this painting, done in 1600–1601 for the Cerasi Chapel, Caravaggio used light to convey the vision that blinded the Apostle.

The Madonna di Loreto

The model for this virgin, painted about 1604, was probably Caravaggio's mistress, the prostitute "Lena, who stands in Piazza Navona . . . Michelangelo's girl."

Supper at Emmaus

Painted in 1601-1602 for Marchese Ciriaco Mattei. The beardless Christ shows that Caravaggio was aware of the fashionable new interest in early Christian art.

Portrait of a Knight of Malta

Painted in 1607–1608 during Caravaggio's novitiate at Valletta, the Knight has recently been identified as Fra' Antonio Martelli, Prior of Messina.

St. Jerome

Painted in 1607–1608, either in Naples or on Malta, for Fra' Ippolito Malaspina, Prior of Naples, whose head was the model for St. Jerome's and who played a key role in helping Caravaggio to become a Knight of Malta.

Alof de Wignancourt, Grand Master of the Order of Malta

Painted in 1607–1608 when Caravaggio was a novice. Fra' Alof had a high opinion of the artist's "burning zeal" for the order, and helped him escape after his arrest.

Beheading of St. John

Painted on Malta during the summer of 1608, this was Caravaggio's "passage money," paid on becoming a Knight. His only known signature is written in blood: "F. Michel A——" —Fra' Michelangelo. Grand Master de Wignancourt rewarded him with a gold chain and two slaves.

Raising of Lazarus

Painted at Messina in 1609, when Caravaggio was on the run in Sicily after fleeing from Malta. He made two workmen hold up a corpse for him to paint, by threatening them with his dagger.

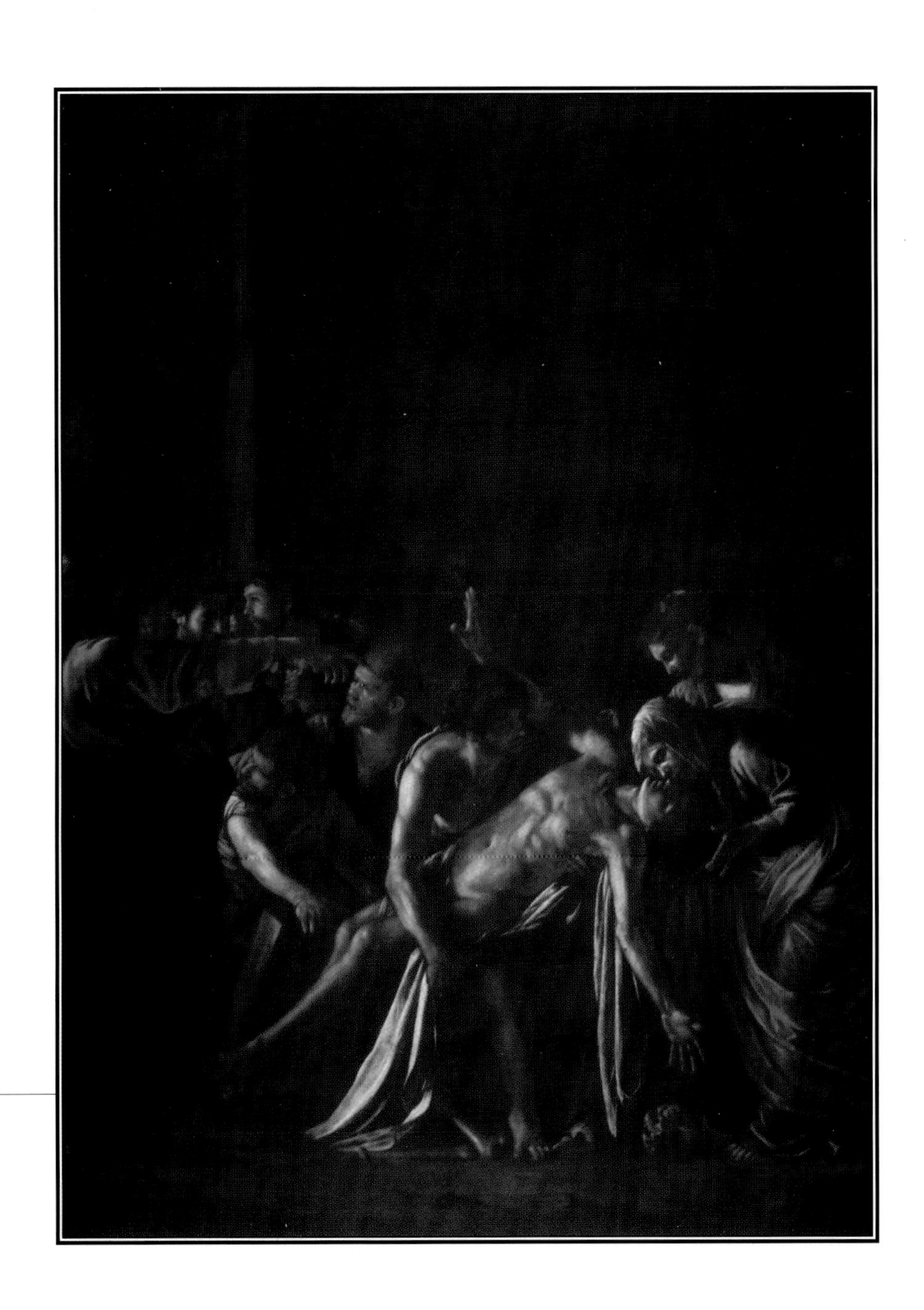

David with the Head of Goliath

A double self-portrait painted while hiding in Naples in 1609–1610. A young, redeemed Caravaggio holds up the head of a sinful, middle-aged Caravaggio.

Castello, where the Commedia del Arte was played, in the gardens at Poggioreale, or on the pleasure boats bound for Posillipo.

Despite its gaiety, life at Naples had sinister undertones. When roused, the mob could be one of the most savage in Europe. There was also a slave market, dealing mainly in North Africans or Turks, though Christians, too, might become slaves. Down by the seafront, Fynes Moryson saw "a stone upon which many play away their liberty at dice, the King's officers lending them money, which, when they have lost and cannot repay, they are drawne into the gallies, for the Spaniards have slaves of both sexes." Girls were sold into prostitution by starving parents, boys for emasculation as *castrato* singers. Those who could afford it mummified their relatives when they died and visited them in the catacombs on feast days.

It was an even more dangerous city than Rome. "The Neapolitane carrieth the bloodiest mind and is the most secret fleering murdrer," warns Thomas Nashe, "whereupon it is growen to a common proverbe, Ile give him the Neapolitane shrug, when one intends to play the villaine, and make no boast of it." Great nobles maintained a much larger number of *bravi* in their palaces, and the surrounding countryside held more *banditti* than the entire Papal States. While duels of the kind in which Ranuccio Tommasoni had died were comparatively rare in Rome, they took place almost every day in Naples.

Popular religion was fervent and dramatic. After the viceroy, the most important person in Naples was the archbishop, who presided over the liquefaction of the blood of San Gennaro, a fourth-century martyr. The congealed blood, contained in two vials, turned to liquid three times a year, and the well-being of Naples depended upon it doing so as quickly as possible. In Caravaggio's day, when the vials of blood were held up at the cathedral by the archbishop, many of the crowd fell into a panic-stricken frenzy, howling and shrieking if the liquefaction were delayed for even a few minutes.

XXIII

The Neapolitan Altarpieces

Caravaggio's fame preceded him. When he arrived, instead of being greeted as a murderer on the run, he was lionized. Later, Bernardo de Dominicis, a seventeenth-century historian of Neapolitan artists, heard how "Caravaggio came to Naples where he was received with great acclaim by both painters and lovers of painting."

All we know about his earliest Neapolitan commission, signed in October 1606, is from the document itself. The patron was Nicholas Radolovich, a merchant from Bari. The commission, an altarpiece, was to show the Virgin and Child with choirs of angels above, St. Dominic embracing St. Francis in the center below, and St. Vitus on the left and St. Nicholas on the right, St. Nicholas being the patron saint of Bari. Like other lost Caravaggios, the painting may still survive unrecognized in the dusty corridor of an obscure religious house, or in a crumbling palace in the Mezzogiorno.

Caravaggio painted three more altarpieces. For the first, *The Seven Works of Mercy,* he charged the confraternity of the Pio Monte della Misericordia twice what he had charged Radolovich. Clearly, he had soon realized how much he was appreciated at Naples. Working with his usual speed, he delivered it by January 1607, when he was paid the final instalment of the four hundred ducats stipulated. Bellori gives us a good description: "The head of an old man is seen, pushed through the bars of a prison window, sucking the milk from a lady who bends down to offer him her naked breast. Among the other figures are the feet and legs of a dead man, who is being taken off for burial; a torch held by someone carrying the body casts its light so as to shine over a priest in a white surplice, to brighten up all the colors and breathe life into the picture."

The young woman and the old man, who represent the Christian mercies of feeding the hungry and visiting prisoners, were inspired by the ancient story of Pero contriving to feed her father, Cimon, when Valerius Maximus tried to starve him to death. Also in the picture are Samson drinking from the jawbone of an ass, St. Martin dividing his cloak, and a host greeting Christ, who is dressed as a pilgrim. Two angels fly above, while the Madonna and Child look down upon the scene. The Virgin has a face not unlike that of the *Madonna di Loreto.* Tense and worried, it may be the face of Lena from the Piazza Navona, who inspired such passion in Caravaggio and could have followed him to Naples.

St. Martin's sword belt and scabbard, painted in some detail, are of considerable value for historians of the rapier. The artist lost none of his interest in swords, even though it is likely that he still felt remorse at killing Tommasoni. There is no record of his falling foul of the Neapolitan authorities, no police report of nocturnal brawls. Chastened by having been hunted for his life, he was on his best behavior.

Another altarpiece, *The Madonna of the Rosary,* seems to have been rejected. It was on sale in Naples in the autumn of 1607, together with a new version of *Judith and Holofernes.* Some believe that in the *Madonna* the donor kneeling at the side, a bald-headed old gentleman in a ruff, is Don Marzio Colonna, Caravaggio's shadowy and slightly sinister host in the Sabine Hills. Because Dominican friars dominate this triumphant painting, there is reason to think that it was painted during the early months of 1607, a time of expectation for the friars.

Their archenemy was the Jesuit General Claudio Acquaviva, the same man who had declined to commission Caravaggio to paint the Resurrection at the Gesù. The Dominicans accused the Jesuits of watering down Catholicism, of stressing the human at the expense of the divine, and of doing so in every area from sexuality to theology. What angered them most was the Jesuit emphasis on free will instead of grace. A series of acrimonious debates on the subject had recently taken place in Rome.

Pope Clement VIII had distrusted Acquaviva, because he was building a worldwide organization, directed from his headquarters at the Gesù. The pope suspected the Society of Jesus of trying to become a church within the Church. He had taken a keen personal interest in the debates on free will versus grace, which might well have ended in general agreement on the need to suppress, or at least drastically curb, the Jesuits. But Clement died before he could give his verdict. Pope Paul V ordered further debates. Soon it began to look as if he, too, were about to condemn the Jesuits.

The Dominicans maintained the Augustinian view that a man was saved more by his faith than his good works, an idea that, the Jesuits claimed, verged on Protestantism. If Caravaggio inclined to the Dominican view, as seems likely from his portrayal of grace as blinding light in *The Conversion of St. Paul,* it provides a rare insight into his mind. This was certainly a comforting doctrine for a man who, despite deep Christian faith, was always prone to spectacular sins.

Throughout the spring and summer of 1607, the Dominicans were confident they would win the dispute and crush the Jesuits. However, at the last moment, the Jesuits managed to ingratiate themselves with Pope Paul, by providing highly effective support during a quarrel that suddenly broke out between the papacy and Venice. Most unexpectedly, in August Paul adjourned the debates indefinitely. There is a very strong possibility, therefore, that the *Madonna of the Rosary* was prematurely commissioned by an enthusiastic supporter of the Dominicans to celebrate their forthcoming victory over the Jesuits. The legend depicted in the painting shows the Virgin presenting St. Dominic with a rosary in a vision, after which he gives rosaries to all his friars. It was an ideal theme for proclaiming the order's triumph, the underlying message being that salvation is best found through Dominican guidance.

An altarpiece was also ordered by Tommaso and Lorenzo dei Franchis, members of an influential Neapolitan family related to the viceroy. They wanted the picture for their new chapel in the church of San Domenico Maggiore. This was the *Flagellation of Christ,* apparently completed and delivered by May 1607, for which Caravaggio was paid 290 ducats. The three figures around the column—Christ and the two men scourging him—have a curious rhythm that has been fancifully called "balletic," and likened to a ritual dance of death. It is among Caravaggio's most savage compositions, a scene of agony and horror. However, the impression that remains with one is not so much of the artist's unhealthy pleasure in cruelty as of his genuine compassion for the suffering Lord.

Caravaggio did not restrict himself to altarpieces during his comparatively short stay in Naples. A *Crucifixion of St. Andrew* was commissioned by the Spanish viceroy himself. Once again, Caravaggio was finding patrons among the highest in the land.

According to *The Golden Legend*, the apostle Andrew angered the Roman proconsul Aegeus by converting his wife, Maximilla, to Christianity. When, after a savage cross-examination, Andrew refused to sacrifice to the idols, he was crucified. For two days he hung on the cross, preaching. When the crowd saw that he was still alive on the third day, they threatened to kill the proconsul if he did not take him down. Alarmed, Aegeus hastened to do as they said. The apostle, however, refused to be taken down, beseeching God to let him stay on the cross. After he had prayed, "a dazzling light came down from Heaven and enveloped him for the space of half an hour, hiding him from sight, and when the light vanished, he breathed forth his soul." As for the miserable proconsul, *The Golden Legend* tells us that on the way home he was "seized by a demon" and died in the street.

It must have been the heavenly light, the light of glory, so well suited to the chiaroscuro, that inspired Caravaggio. It illumines not only the dying St. Andrew but the amazed faces of those gazing up at him—Aegeus in an elegant armor and plumed headgear, a rapt old woman with a goiter, a gaping peasant in a broad-brimmed hat—and the bare back of the executioner, who is vainly trying to take the apostle down from the cross with trembling hands.

When the viceroy left Naples in 1610, he took the *Crucifixion of St. Andrew* home with him to Spain, where it disappeared. It was rediscovered in Madrid less than thirty years ago.

XXIV

The Prior of Naples

We do not know exactly how Caravaggio became a Knight of Malta, but the circumstances suggest that Fra' Ippolito Malaspina, Prior of Naples, had a good deal to do with it. Although there is no documentary evidence that he supported the artist's candidacy, he was the logical person in the city to advise him about how to join the order. His head may have been the model for that of another *St. Jerome,* painted by Caravaggio either at Naples or on Malta. If so, we have a remarkable idea of the impression he made on Caravaggio, who, presumably working from memory, portrayed a tough veteran in his sixties, with very strong features and impressive serenity.

Caravaggio could well have met him at Rome, in the company of his brother-in-law, Ottavio Costa, and would have noticed his voluminous black "choir mantle" with a large, eight-pointed white cross on the shoulder, and his cloth-of-gold surcoat. He was called "Fra' " because, like all his brethren, he had taken the vows of poverty, chastity, and obedience. Not a Neapolitan but a Tuscan marquis from the Lunigiana, born in 1544, he had entered the Order of Malta when very young yet, despite fighting heroically at Lepanto, he had only recently emerged as one of its most influential members, after the election of his friend Alof de Wignancourt as grand master in 1601.

Appointed prior of Naples the following year, he had relinquished his priory on taking command of the papal fleet, but was reinstated in October 1606, less than a month after Caravaggio reached the city. Neapolitan grandees took care to be on good terms with him, since, as prior, he ranked among the great dignitaries of Naples.

Throughout Italy the knights were popular to the point of adulation as the finest fighting seamen in the world. They guarded the peninsula's coastline against Turks and North African slave raiders, their galleys patrolling the Mediterranean and attacking Muslim ships wherever they found them. Crusading ideals still meant something in the seventeenth century, and it was no accident that Tasso's *Gerusalemme Liberata* should have been a poetic evocation of the First Crusade. What made the order even more imposing was that its warrior-monks were nearly all aristocrats, admitted as Knights of Justice only after providing cast-iron proofs of patrician ancestry. Even the few non-noble knights, or Knights of Grace, had to be men of distinction.

Sandrart and, by inference, Vincenzo Giustiniani, were both convinced that Caravaggio had planned to become a Knight of Malta before leaving Rome. Bellori, however, has a different story. "Caravaggio was desirous of receiving the cross of Malta, which is generally given by grace to men who are thought worthy because of their merit and quality. So he decided to go to the island, where he was presented to the Grand Master." But it seems most unlikely that Caravaggio would ever have gone to Malta without an assurance that he would be accepted for the order's novitiate.

The idea of an artist entering the order was not such a fantasy as it sounds. Caravaggio's friend Ludovico Cardi, "Il Cigoli," joined the order in 1613, and later Mattia Preti was a triumphant success as a painter-knight. Significantly, Il Cigoli owed his admission to Cardinal Borghese, who wanted to reward him for decorating his Roman villa. The grand master was always anxious to oblige the cardinal secretary, and Borghese could easily have done Caravaggio the same service. Although no firm proof exists, it is likely that he played a much greater part in Caravaggio's career than has been realized.

He was certainly the right person through whom to obtain a papal dispensation for a murderer to enter the order.

Caravaggio had much to offer the knights, who wanted the best paintings in Europe. They did not wish their churches to be in any way inferior to those of the Jesuits or the Oratorians, and they had more ready money. The grand master knew all about the killing of Ranuccio Tommasoni, but did not see it as an obstacle. He was used to dealing with duelists. Given the customs of a violent age and the fact they were professional soldiers, more than a few of his knights besides the Marchesa Costanza's son had killed an opponent in a duel. As for Caravaggio's notorious temper, Fra' Alof had plenty of experience in handling the haughtiest and most pugnacious body of men in the entire Mediterranean.

Caravaggio's lack of pedigree was a much more serious problem. The knights had recently become stricter about "noble proofs," since too many young men were trying to join. Fortunately, the statutes allowed the grand master to let a few non-noble candidates enter the order as Knights of Grace (or "Obedience"). He did so sparingly, because admissions often infuriated the nobly born Knights of Justice. Their wrath was however generally reserved for blatant social climbers, especially those who were Genoese. In Caravaggio's case, as Francesco Susinno put it, the aspirant knight "was admired by everyone in the Order on account of his skill with a brush, and they all wanted his pictures."

There must have been a lot of paperwork concerning Caravaggio's candidacy. At some stage, Fra' Alof agreed formally to his coming to Malta and trying his vocation. Although he was thirty-five, for a year the artist would have to submit to all the petty restrictions of a novitiate and obey a novice master. His readiness to do so shows just how anxious he was to become a Knight of Malta.

XXV

The Knights of Malta, July 1607

Just after midsummer 1607, the galleys of Malta sailed into the Bay of Naples, their first visit for over a year. Red-hulled and gilded, with huge triangular lateen sails of striped canvas, flying silk banners, these gorgeous warships were commanded by the knights' senior fighting officer at sea, the Captain-General of the Galleys. This was Fra' Fabrizio Sforza Colonna, the Marchesa Costanza's son. His fleet was bound for Genoa before returning to Malta, and Caravaggio sailed with him.

The galleys were the fastest ships in the Mediterranean, but, built for speed with long, narrow hulls, they pitched and rolled horribly. They were also overcrowded, each carrying nearly five hundred soldiers, sailors, and oarsmen, and contagious fevers often broke out among the filthy, verminous galley slaves. Caravaggio must have sailed with the dozen red-surcoated knights on the poop deck, sheltered to some extent from sun and rain by a red canvas awning. Even for knights, however, life on board a galley was uncomfortable. No food could be cooked in such cramped quarters, the fleet putting into a harbor every few days to take on food and water. Their only relaxations were cards and dice. When the ship rowed into the wind, the knights plugged their noses against the stench from the oarsmen chained at their benches. Above the crash of oars, a drum beat out the time and the *Aguzzino,* or overseer, could be heard cracking his whip. Each galley carried a chaplain, oars being shipped for morning prayers, while the *Angelus* was said at noon and in the evening. Weather permitting, Mass was celebrated on the poop.

The fleet put in briefly at Livorno and other ports, just long enough for Caravaggio to enjoy a hot meal. The voyage home would have been by way of Corsica, Sardinia, and Sicily. Its main purpose was to look out for the Barbary corsairs, operating from Algiers, Tunis, or Tripoli, who preyed on Christian merchantmen or raided for slaves along the Italian coastline. If the knights sighted a corsair, they could usually run her down, and it is not impossible that Caravaggio saw a naval action of this sort. His voyage would have been still more uncomfortable if Fra' Fabrizio's ships had to ride out one of those frightening Mediterranean storms that even in summer can blow up without warning.

At last the fleet sighted the rocky coast of Malta, and then Caravaggio caught his first glimpse of Valletta on the ridge of Monte Sceberras—a long beak of rock running out into the middle of a great bay, which it divided into two natural harbors. It is probable that he landed here on 12 July 1607.

The two things most people knew about Malta were that a great apostle was shipwrecked on it, "where the viper leapt on Paul's hand," and that it was ruled by the knights. Being in the center of the Mediterranean, it had always been of strategic importance, and at the same time vulnerable to seaborne raids. When the knights arrived in 1530, they found most of the inhabitants talking "a sort of Moorish" but ruled by an Italian-speaking aristocracy with titles from the kings of Sicily. By Caravaggio's time, the population had risen to about fifty thousand, the nobles living in the former capital, Citta Notabile—today called Mdina.

The Order of St. John of Jerusalem had been founded in the eleventh century, to shelter pilgrims to the holy land, taking up arms to defend them. When the Latin East fell to Islam, the "Knights Hospitaller" moved to

Rhodes and then to Malta, which they held from the king of Spain (as king of Sicily) in return for the gift of a falcon every All Saints' Day. They were justly admired for their heroism in 1565 when, hopelessly outnumbered, they had beaten off a Turkish invasion, which many still remembered when Caravaggio arrived on the island. Ever since the Great Siege, the knights had been building their new capital, "Valletta Humilissima."

There were about eighteen hundred knights, of whom less than half lived on Malta. They were monks as well as knights, vowing to be poor in spirit, chaste, and obedient, confessing and taking Communion frequently, especially before going into battle, and reciting daily the Little Office of Our Lady. Death in combat against the infidel, whether boarding a Barbary corsair or raiding a Turkish seaport, was regarded as martyrdom.

The sea "caravans" of the knights brought them rich rewards. Entering their houses in Valletta, Caravaggio would have found Oriental rugs, chests of rare eastern woods, Chinese porcelain, and massive services of silver plate. However, many brethren left the island after they had sailed on enough caravans to qualify them for promotion, each returning to an often palatial commandery on the European mainland, to spend the rest of his life running its estates and sending its revenues out to Malta.

Besides the knights' crusading vocation, there was that of the Hospitaller, of caring for "Our Lords the Sick." The Sacred Infirmary held over 350 beds, employed several teams of doctors, and was better equipped than any contemporary hospital in Europe. But although the brethren visited it on certain specified days, it was almost impossible for them to live both callings. Even so, a few knights nursed at the infirmary on a regular basis, at least one specializing in the care of sick galley slaves. Brethren of this sort led a monastic existence, living permanently in a retreat house at Valletta, the Camerata.

During the 1590s, the Abbé de Brantôme observed of the then grand master, "he is revered almost as a king, and everyone defers to him as if he really was one, addressing him with the utmost humility and always with the head bared." In the year Caravaggio came to Malta, the Holy Roman Emperor created Fra' Alof and his successors Princes of Malta and Gozo. However, another of his titles was "Guardian of the Poor of Jesus Christ," and at his installation a silken cord and scrip (or pilgrim's satchel) was fastened around his waist in token of his duty to help them. First and foremost, the grand master was a spiritual superior.

Whether they concentrated on their crusader or on their Hospitaller vocations, the brethren were in the last analysis monks as well as knights, and when Caravaggio joined them he must have known very well that he was entering a religious order.

XXVI

The Novice, 1607–1608

The first mention of Caravaggio on Malta is during an investigation by the Inquisition into the rumored bigamy of an unnamed Greek artist. On 14 July 1607, Caravaggio had been a guest in a knight's house at Valletta when the Greek was present. He was questioned by Paolo Cassar, an official of the "General Inquisitor for Heretical Depravity." "I don't know anything about what your most reverend lordship is asking me, except that there was a Greek painter staying at Fra' Giacomo Marchese's residence and that he arrived here on the galleys a fortnight ago," Caravaggio told him. "I'm aware of nothing that ought to be reported to the Holy Office about this knight, or about anyone else, and I don't know where the painter came from."

A novice, he was technically *in convento,* living as if he were in a monastery. Most of the seven Langues into which the order was divided had their own fortress-like *auberge,* in Caravaggio's case the Auberge of Italy. It housed the novices and younger knights, who slept in cubicles and dined in its refectory. Because of his age, he was probably allowed to lodge with a knight in Valletta, but he would have had to dine at the *auberge,* besides attending church services and lectures with the other novices; led by a senior knight, they said the Little Office together daily and recited the Rosary, visiting the infirmary once a week to nurse "Our Lords the Sick." They also received instruction in seamanship, gunnery, and fencing. Presumably Caravaggio was excused from these, though not classes on the statutes, customs, and traditions of the "Religion," the brethren's name for their order.

The Master of the Novices, their spiritual adviser, was Don Giovanni Bertolotti, a chaplain of the order. A distinguished theologian from Bologna, as the grand master's confessor he had great influence. During his term of office, the Oratory of St. John was built onto the conventual church, specifically for the novices' use. In addition, Caravaggio must have had the guidance of a senior knight from the Langue of Italy. Probably this was Fra' Antonio Martelli. In 1966 a portrait of a Knight of Malta at the Pitti Palace in Florence was identified as Caravaggio's work. At first the sitter was thought to be Wignancourt, but recent research has established that it is Fra' Antonio. A Florentine born in 1534, he had fought so bravely during the Great Siege that Grand Master de la Vallette rewarded him with a rich commandery. He received rapid promotion when Wignancourt became grand master, appointed prior of Messina, one of the Langue of Italy's key posts. Caravaggio's portrait shows a battered if well-preserved old noble with a cropped head and a faded red beard. Despite his scraggy neck, the weathered, sunburned face is alarmingly formidable, with a tight mouth and very shrewd eyes.

We do not know how often Fra' Ippolito Malaspina came over from Naples, but he was on Malta in February 1608. Possibly it was then that Caravaggio painted, or at least finished, the *St. Jerome.* Although some think St. Jerome's face may be the grand master's, it is almost certainly the prior's, since the artist has added the Malaspina arms at the bottom right-hand corner, a thornbush in flower. Recently restored, the picture now hangs in the Oratory of St. John. Cleaning has brought back the dazzling light in which Caravaggio clothed the saint, the light of divine inspiration.

If there was never any chance of Caravaggio going to sea to fight the Turks, apparently he sympathized with his brethren's crusader ideals. Sandrart claims that he "generously equipped a carrack," though the enormous sum required would clearly have been beyond his resources. It is more likely that he contributed to the fund that the grand master was amassing to build a big, new square-rigged warship, a carrack, for the religion's navy.

Malta was far from being a "dreary isle," as Howard Hibbard calls it. Before the knights' arrival, it had resembled a miniature Sicily even if most of the population spoke Maltese. Its cities looked like Sicilian or Italian cities, particularly the new capital at Valletta, while the order's international membership made it "an epitome of all Europe." The seamen and merchants, Italians, Greeks, Armenians, and Jews, who swarmed in its ports, added to the cosmopolitan air. Although stony and largely treeless, the landscape was not unpleasing. Admittedly the sweltering summers were trying, an unpleasant sirocco blowing in August. "They here stir early and late, in regard of the immoderate heat, and sleep at the noonday," reports Sandys. Throughout the winter there were gales and high seas. But, accustomed to Rome and Naples, Caravaggio can have found little difficulty in coping with the climate.

Valletta, where Caravaggio spent most of his time, was a handsome city of yellow limestone, a grid of smart streets behind massive fortifications. Although the Auberge of Italy, now the General Post Office, was bombed during the Second World War, he would still recognize its sculpted facade and great Baroque entrance, its spacious courtyard around a well surmounted by a high arch; next door stood the Italian Langue's own church, dedicated to St. Catherine of Italy. As a novice, he had to be in St. John's church, just round the corner from the Auberge, almost every day. No other buildings, not even the Contarelli Chapel, have such close associations with him.

When not at sea, the life of a knight was comfortable, even luxurious, with Turkish or North African slaves to wait on him. The cuisine was world-famous, first-class cooks being brought from Europe, while fine wines were imported, together with snow from Mount Etna to cool them. Social amusements consisted of a never-ending round of receptions and card parties in richly furnished apartments or shady gardens. There were concerts and sometimes plays at the Auberges. There were also temptations. Sandys writes of "the number of allowed curtizans (for the most part Grecians) who sit playing in their doors on instruments; and with the art of their eyes inveigle those continent by vow." There do not seem to have been many models among them, judging from the lack of young women in Caravaggio's painting while he was on the island. In any case, he himself was preparing to become continent by vow.

Apart from going to sea on a "caravan," the most dangerous thing a knight could do was to quarrel with one of his brethren. Confined on their little island, they were prone to fall out and settle disputes in the manner of their class, by dueling, although fatalities were rare. The statutory penalty for fighting a duel was "Loss of the Habit," expulsion from the order, but usually lesser punishments were imposed if nobody had been killed or badly wounded. Yet for over a year there is no record of Caravaggio quarreling. He was well aware that as a novice he was on probation. It is also likely that he went in awe of those three grim old men, the grand master and the priors of Messina and Naples.

Malta gave Caravaggio a new country and a new identity. The island was a sovereign state and, as *Malta Gerosolomitana,* heir of the old crusader states in Palestine. What it lacked in size, it made up for in prestige; for an Italian, there was no more honorable profession than that of a "Jerusalem Knight" (or *Cavaliere Gerosolomitano*). And membership conferred nobility on those without blue blood, which cannot have displeased a painter of ill-defined social standing. No doubt he enjoyed the company too. If men of the sword, the knights were by no means Philistines. Many were younger sons of immensely wealthy families, who had grown up in palaces, surrounded by beautiful possessions. This was especially true of the Italian Langue, more than a few of whose members would have known great painting when they saw it. They had genuine respect for so magnificent an artist, while he himself must have been deeply flattered by their acceptance and at the prospect of joining them. Above all, he enjoyed the warm approval of the grand master, Fra' Alof. The time that Caravaggio spent on Malta may well have been the happiest of his entire life.

The Grand Master

One of the knights' ablest and most likable rulers, Caravaggio's grand master, Fra' Alof de Wignancourt, had been born in Artois in 1547. Although he did not come out to Malta until 1566, a year after the Great Siege, he had served under the legendary Grand Master de la Vallette, who made him Captain of Valletta with special responsibility for guarding the order's new capital while it was being built. After completing his caravans at sea, he had gone home to run a commandery in the dangerous France of the Wars of Religion, returning to Malta as Hospitaller in 1597.

As soon as Fra' Alof was elected grand master in 1601, it became clear that an innovator was in charge. He put real vigor into the knights' crusade against the infidel, their galleys raiding Greece, Turkey, Syria, and North Africa, bringing back impressive booty together with quantities of slaves. Anxious to enhance the pomp and grandeur of his office, he established a corps of twelve pages, aspirant novices, to wait on him. In 1611 George Sandys noted, "For albeit a Frier (as the rest of the Knights), yet is he an absolute Soveraigne, and is bravely attended on by a number of gallant yong Gentlemen." He chose them from the poorer nobility, paying for their education himself.

Wignancourt took good care of his Maltese subjects, much better than any shown by his predecessors. Formerly, whole families of country people had been dragged off to the Moorish slave markets by Barbary corsairs, on one occasion the neighboring island of Gozo's entire population, so he built small forts where they could take shelter from raiders, besides setting up a bank for ransoming captives. The Maltese, who idolized him, thought he was a wizard, which probably means that, like del Monte, he took an active interest in alchemy.

For all his fire-eating appearance in Caravaggio's famous portrait at the Louvre, Fra' Alof was a pleasant, modest man, genuinely benevolent, and gifted with exceptional tact. Despite his firm leadership and his innovations, he was never autocratic or overbearing, never attempted to rule as an absolute monarch, "Very easy to do business with, always open to suggestions before taking a decision, always ready to listen to the opinions of the experts on both civil and military matters," writes the historian dall' Pozzo, who had obviously spoken to elderly knights who remembered his reign. "He chose extremely well qualified officers and counselors, ruling with their advice and taking careful account of their views. . . . Among his principal advisers was the Bailiff of Naples, Fra' Ippolito Malaspina."

Every grand master made the painful discovery that he had extremely difficult subjects to govern. The main disturbance during Caravaggio's time on Malta came from the Langue of Germany. In 1607 uproar broke out among the German knights when they learned that Fra' Alof had given permission for the Comte de Brie, a bastard son of the Duke of Lorraine, to join the German Langue. There was a long and noisy dispute. At one point the enraged Germans pulled down the arms of the grand master and the Religion from their accustomed place over the main gateway of the Langue of Germany. Eventually, Fra' Alof was forced to give in, arranging for the count to be admitted into the much less demanding Langue of Italy, where he became a novice with Caravaggio. The Italians were nearly always prepared to accept a papal dispensation for inadequate proofs of nobility, and the grand master must have asked Scipione Borghese to provide one for Brie.

The Comte de Brie's story shows Wignancourt's ability to compromise and his diplomatic finesse at using Rome. It also underlines the extraordinary emphasis placed by the Religion on the value of impeccably noble birth, and in the very uneasy position in which painters of obscure origin might find themselves if they became Knights of Malta. Brie should have been a warning to Caravaggio.

The grand master was in frequent contact with the cardinal nephew, through the Religion's ambassador at Rome. He needed his support constantly in dealing with such problems as the Inquisitor, who saw himself as unofficial papal nuncio to Malta. Knights in trouble for some offense often appealed through him to the pope against the order's sentence, so that his meddling was an endless source of vexation. Fra' Alof had every reason to keep on good terms with Borghese, whose weakness for Caravaggio made Wignancourt no doubt still more inclined to like the artist.

Even so, Fra' Alof's primary motive was to use Caravaggio in the service of the Religion. He had seen Valletta rise from the ground and now he wanted to make it as beautiful as possible. Probably while he was still in the novitiate, Caravaggio produced not less than three portraits of Fra' Alof. The first, now at the Louvre and the only one to survive, shows him in a splendid, gold-inlaid ceremonial armor, grasping an admiral's baton. The second portrait has disappeared, although there is a clumsy copy at Rabat; it depicted Fra' Alof as hospitaller instead of crusader, wearing his choir mantle and seated at a desk on which there were a crucifix and a book of hours. The third, a head and shoulders, is known only from a French engraving of 1609. Was the grand master aware that Caravaggio had painted the pope, and is that perhaps why he sat for him so many times?

During the sittings, Fra' Alof had plenty of opportunity to speak with the artist, and obviously he could see no reason to change his mind about admitting him to the Religion. After only a few months, the grand master decided that his protégé definitely possessed a vocation to become a Knight of Malta. On 29 December 1607, he wrote two letters, one to the order's amabassador at Rome, Fra' Francesco Lomellini, and the other to its former ambassador, Fra' Giacomo Bosio, asking them to obtain a papal dispensation to enter the Religion for someone who had committed a murder. No letter to the omnipotent Cardinal Borghese survives, but it would have been unthinkable not to seek his help.

On 7 February 1608, the grand master formally petitioned the pope for a dispensation, "on this occasion only, to clothe and adorn with a Magistral Knight's habit two persons of whom he has a very high opinion and whom he is nominating, although one of them has committed a homicide during a street brawl." There must have been a good deal of discreet lobbying before Fra' Alof presented the petition. Again, it is likely that the cardinal secretary played a key role behind the scenes. No names are mentioned in the petition, but it is inconceivable that Rome remained unaware of the murderer's identity. The grand master was far too shrewd to risk trying to deceive the Curia, let alone Pope Paul.

Rome was notoriously slow at answering petitions, yet somebody, presumably Borghese, made sure that the pontiff answered at once. On February 15, he sent a papal "brief" to Malta, granting Wignancourt's request, while warning that it was a special case that must not be seen as creating a precedent.

In July, Fra' Alof issued a magistral bull, commanding that "the honorable Michelangelo of Caracca in Lombardy, in the vernacular called 'Caravaggio,'" should be admitted into the Order of Malta as a Knight of Magistral Obedience, because of "his burning zeal for the Religion . . . and his great desire to be clothed with the habit."

XXVIII

"Fra' Michelangelo," July 1608

The great monument to Michelangelo da Caravaggio's dream of becoming a Knight of Malta is still to be seen in the procathedral at Valletta, formerly the order's conventual church. It is the *Beheading of St. John the Baptist,* the most magnificent of all his paintings. It is peculiarly personal in that it enshrines his devoted allegiance to the Religion.

John the Baptist was the knights' protector in the holy land, on Rhodes and on Malta, as he remains today. On more than one occasion his sudden appearance in the sky, accompanied by the Virgin, announced triumph over apparently hopeless odds. The *Vittoria* Mass on 8 September (the Feast of the Virgin's Nativity) was one of the greatest days in the order's calendar. Everyone on Malta believed the Turks had abandoned the Great Siege on that day in 1565, leaving the knights victorious, because they had seen the Baptist and the Virgin in the clouds, coming to the brethren's rescue. The "Victory" Mass has been said ever since. In Caravaggio's time the Religion marched through Valletta, the prior bearing the icon of Our Lady of Philermo—its most cherished relic—while during Mass the grand master brandished the sword presented to Vallette by King Philip II, and from the city walls cannon fired salute after salute.

The Baptist sailed into battle with the knights, his gilded statue at the poop of every galley and his head on their banners. His likeness was engraved on many of the brethren's breastplates, helmets, swords, and daggers. Several times a year his hand, cased in silver, was borne in procession around the conventual church.

The Religion's greatest feast was St. John's Nativity on 24 June. During the week before, all seagoing was suspended; no boat would leave the harbor till it was over. At the vigil on the previous day, the knights heard how John's father had prophesied that the Last of the Prophets "shall convert many of the children of Israel to the Lord their God." On the feast itself, all the brethren on the island were present at Mass in the conventual church, when the sermon extolled the holy war against the foes of the risen Christ, promising salvation to all who died fighting in it or as captives of the infidel. The rest of the day, apart from vespers, was given up to banqueting, regattas, and fireworks.

Caravaggio could have chosen no subject with a greater impact on the Knights of Malta than the Beheading of St. John the Baptist, nor could anything have fascinated him more, given his own ghastly obsession with decapitation. As usual, Bellori has a good description, having traveled to Malta to see the painting, which Caravaggio probably completed while he was still a novice: "The saint has fallen to the ground while the executioner, as though he had not been able to cut it off at once with his sword, takes his knife from his side in order to sever the head from the trunk. Herodias is looking on intently, while the jailer, dressed as a Turk, points fiercely at this awful butchery." Caravaggio had succeeded in finding just the right model, beautiful and auburn haired, for Herodias, who holds the charger in readiness for her daughter's gruesome reward. Perhaps she was one of the Greek courtesans who shocked Sandys.

The largest of his pictures, it must have been painted where it was to hang, in the recently completed Oratory of San Giovanni Decollato in the conventual church, as an altarpiece between the Doric pillars on the east wall. The oratory was used as a lecture hall for the novices, and was more than familiar to him. Here he spent the night before taking his vows, in vigil before what many consider his masterpiece. It was his *passagio* or passage money, the sum paid by every Knight on entering the Religion.

Understandably, Caravaggio was pleased with this painting, the only one he is known to have signed, "F Michelangelo." It is not clear if he signed it before or after his profession; he may well have done so afterward, proud of at last being able to call himself "Fra' Michelangelo." The signature is in blood, or at any rate blood red, as if lifeblood streaming from the Baptist's neck. The head is not a self-portrait. Even Caravaggio dared not shock his new brethren in such a way.

The painting's impact on the Religion, especially on the grand master, was overwhelming. We have to remember the knights' intense devotion to their conventual church, whose decoration was the first item in the order's annual budget. So far, it was a starkly functional building, largely unadorned, and therefore an unrivaled setting for so dramatic a painting.

Caravaggio took his vows at Mass in the Oratory on 14 July 1608, between the Epistle and the Gospel, in front of his own painting of St. John. Having confessed his sins, wearing a red silk surcoat embroidered with a great white cross, he stood before Fra' Alof. First, he was made a knight. At the Giving of the Sword, he was reminded that normally membership of the Religion was "by custom granted only to those who, by virtue of their ancient lineage and personal virtue, are accounted worthy." He promised to defend the Church, together with "those who are poor, dispossessed, orphaned, sick and suffering." Next, he was clothed as a monk, swearing on the crucifix to obey his superiors and live in poverty and chastity. He was given the habit, the black choir mantle with a white cross, and a stole embroidered with symbols of the Passion.

The bull for his admission states that Malta would honor him "as the island of Cos honoured its own Apelles," suggesting the document was issued after he had produced some particularly impressive painting, probably the

Beheading of St. John. Bellori says it so delighted Fra' Alof that he gave Caravaggio a gold chain and two slaves as a reward. He was doing just what the grand master had hoped—producing pictures that would shed luster on the Religion.

Even so, judging from his small output on Malta, he seems to have spent comparitively little time painting. Perhaps he had difficulty in finding the right models, though whoever posed for Herodias was a woman of great beauty. Possibly he painted works that await rediscovery. He certainly produced a now-lost portrait of Fra' Ippolito Malaspina, once in Ottavio Costa's collection, which, no doubt, had been commissioned by that discerning patron. A picture that has survived from the Maltese period is a repellent *Sleeping Cupid,* the subject of which, with his swollen stomach, looks more like a dead baby intended as a warning for celibates against the joys of fatherhood. Today in the Galleria Palatina at Florence, it originally belonged to a knight, Fra' Francesco dell' Antella.

Now that he had been professed, he would have time to dazzle his new brethren with his genius. But, if neither noble nor young enough to fight at sea against the infidel, was a painter really suited to the last crusaders' calling? Not everyone on Malta thought so.

The Unknown Knight, September 1608

Caravaggio's career as a Knight of Malta was all too brief, ending suddenly in his arrest and disgrace. We do not have the full details, but we can discount the theory that he was disowned by the order when it learned about the killing of Ranuccio Tommasoni. The grand master had always known this and had obtained a dispensation.

While contemporary sources agree on the broad outlines of what happened, the key account is by Susinno, who wrote a hundred years later. From his vocabulary, it looks as though he himself belonged to the Order of Malta, as either a chaplain or as a Priest of Obedience, that is, a priest employed to serve one of the knights' chapels. He therefore understood the Religion and its members' highly individual mentality. No other early writer on Caravaggio possessed this sort of specialist knowledge.

Bellori's version of Caravaggio's Maltese downfall is, however, the one that has been used most. He says, "abruptly, his disturbed genius caused him to forfeit the Grand Master's favor, and because of a stupid quarrel with a most noble Knight, he was thrown into prison. . . ." Clearly, Bellori had heard that his opponent was someone of considerable distinction.

Susinno's account is not so very different, but it contains one particularly significant clue. "Michelangelo paraded in front of everybody with the Cross on his chest, but this did not calm his troubled spirit, and he let himself be blinded by *the madness of thinking himself a nobleman born* [italics mine]. A Knight's quality is not shown by pride, but by a wish to please. He grew so rash that one day he competed with other Knights, and he fought with a Knight of Justice."

If there was one thing of which every member of the Religion was profoundly convinced, it was the value of noble blood, descent from a long line of warrior aristocrats with unquestioned lordship over the land and those who toiled on it. God had placed all men in the condition He saw fit, and Susinno reflected the general view, that Caravaggio was insane to think himself the equal of a man who was a Knight of Justice by right of noble birth. Generally, other men of obscure origin who became knights through dispensation were gratifyingly mindful of their "low extraction."

Speculation about just what prompted the quarrel has ranged from a dispute over a woman to a sexual assault on one of the grand master's pages, lurid fantasies for which there is not the slightest shred of evidence. The most plausible explanation is undoubtedly Susinno's, that it was a fight over rank and birth. Some years later another painter-knight, Mattia Preti, also a Knight of Magistral Obedience, found himself in a situation of this sort when a member of the Religion began to sneer at his questionable pretensions to noble blood and his undistinguished background. After a few days, Preti lost his temper, whipped out his rapier, and left the man for dead.

Caravaggio's haughty antagonist may well have told him that he was no more than a painter. It was probably a considerable time since anyone had spoken unpleasantly to Fra' Michelangelo. As Bellori put it, Caravaggio "had lived on Malta as an honoured guest, prospering in every way." He had forgotten that he had arrived on the island as a fugitive. The Religion's flattery and his new status as a professed knight had completely turned his head.

We do not know his opponent's name, though Bellori's "most noble

Knight" sounds very like a Bailiff Grand Cross, one of the order's senior officers. It is also possible that he belonged to one of the great families of southern Italy, since he had unusually good contacts in Naples. Clearly very important, and perhaps elderly, he was a man whom Caravaggio should never have dared to confront. The combat that ensued was much more than a brush with swords. No one else seems to have taken part, since no one else was arrested afterward. It looks as though Caravaggio attacked his antagonist in a burst of blind rage. He appears to have hurt him very badly, inflicting wounds that would take months to heal.

Why did the fight cause such outrage among the Religion? Despite the harsh penalties, duels were not uncommon at Valletta, generally taking place in Strada Stretta. It was customary to mark with a cross the spot where a knight had been killed, and during the next century an English tourist counted twenty crosses in this street. What seems to have angered the brethren was not so much Caravaggio fighting a duel as his opponent's distinction.

Instead of rushing down to the harbor, boarding a boat about to sail, and escaping from Malta without delay, Caravaggio simply went home and stayed there, apparently unhurt. What makes his behavior so extraordinary is that, during his novitiate, his novice master must surely have made sure that the killer of Ranuccio Tommasoni learned all about the savage penalties on Malta for this sort of offense. He was quickly arrested by the grand viscount, the island's senior police officer; perhaps significantly, he was not apprehended by the master squire, who normally dealt with errant brethren. Far from being confined to his house, he was immediately dragged off to prison, plainly on orders given at the very highest level.

His arrest by the grand viscount, who seldom had dealings with members of the Religion, was so unusual that everyone in Valletta must have heard about it. Undoubtedly, the order was very angry indeed and wanted to punish him severely. Yet, if it did, it would face an international outcry for imprisoning such a great artist. The grand master was well aware that Scipione Borghese, in particular, could be counted on to make serious trouble, and he had no wish to upset the omnipotent cardinal secretary. Fra' Alof may even have wanted to pardon Caravaggio. He had the power to do so, but, conceivably, he feared that a pardon in this case might upset the brethren. He seems to have decided that the simplest solution was to let the painter escape, and then expel him from the Religion.

Caravaggio had done more than make it impossible for himself to remain a member of the Order of Malta. He had acquired the most dangerous enemy of his entire career. We can be sure of at least one thing about the unknown knight. He was implacably revengeful. When he recovered from his wounds, he would begin a carefully planned vendetta, and Caravaggio would live in fear for his life until the day he died.

A Dungeon Called the "Birdcage," September 1608

Meanwhile, in chains and under armed guard, Caravaggio had been taken by boat across Grand Harbor to the Religion's state prison at Fort Sant' Angelo. Landing, he was marched through a narrow gate, then up steep ramps into the inner castle. On the tip of the peninsula occupied by the city of Vittoriosa, Fort Sant' Angelo was Malta's Bastille, ringed by massive walls and bastions, surrounded by sea on three sides and by a deep moat on the fourth. It was constantly patrolled by sentries on guard against a sudden Turkish attack or a revolt by the slaves. Over the drawbridge, Vittoriosa was almost as closely guarded, its great gates firmly shut each night.

The prisoner Caravaggio was thrown into the fortress's maximum-security cell, a painful experience in itself since the cell was eleven feet deep. He had been in jail many times before, but never in a place like this. Beehive-shaped and about twelve feet in diameter, the *guva*, or "birdcage," had been hacked out of the limestone rock like a well; the only opening was the wellhead at the top, three feet round and closed by an iron grille. If someone gave him a candle before the grille slammed down, he would have been able to see from prayers or coats of arms scratched on the walls that other knights had been imprisoned here already; one sad little inscription referred to "this living grave." Since the *guva* was near a key gateway, opposite the well-attended chapel of Our Lady of Victories, occasionally he could hear footsteps and voices. His horrible prison was stiflingly hot during the autumn days, icy cold at night. Bellori may well be quoting the artist's own words, if at second hand, when he says he was "fearful of an evil end and in terror."

However, Caravaggio spent only a few days in the *guva.* Baglione tells us that "during the night, he climbed out of the prison and fled, reaching the isle of Sicily," while Bellori writes of his "fleeing unrecognized to Sicily, so fast that no one was able to recapture him." It is obvious that in the darkness someone pulled Caravaggio up from out of his dungeon with a rope or a rope ladder and then lowered him over the high walls down to the sea; they also provided him with a safe conduct, so that the sentries of the most closely guarded fortress in the Mediterranean would not shoot at him. A boat was waiting below, because it was much too risky to cross Vittoriosa, whose gates were shut in any case. No one else is known to have got out of the *guva* and escaped from Fort Sant' Angelo. The only possible explanation must be that he was "sprung" by people acting on the instructions of somebody very high up in the order indeed, presumably the grand master himself.

Somehow, Caravaggio mysteriously acquired a large sum of money, enough to hire a felucca and pay its crew sufficiently to risk putting to sea at night, despite the danger from corsairs lurking outside the harbor in the darkness. Bellori and Susinno both say that as soon as he reached Sicily, he went straight to Syracuse, remaining there for some months. Syracuse was the nearest big port to Malta, used by the order's galleys and transports, with an important commandery; it was visited constantly by the knights, who were frequently to be seen in its streets. Not the slightest attempt was made to rearrest him while he was at Syracuse, which serves to confirm the suspicion that Fra' Alof arranged his escape.

On 6 October 1608, the procurator made a formal complaint to the grand master and his council, to the effect that Fra' Michelangelo had fled from Fort Sant' Angelo. This implies he had escaped very recently. In response, Fra' Alof and the council commissioned two knights to seek help from the master squire's men in recapturing him and discovering how he had escaped. Needless to say, they could find no trace of him.

On 7 December, a general assembly of all members of the Religion on Malta was summoned to meet in the Oratory of St. John, to discuss the case formally. A report, now lost, was read to the assembly by the master squire. It stated that Fra' Michelangelo Merisi da Caravaggio "while confined in the prison at Fort Sant' Angelo had escaped from the said fortress by means of ropes" and that, despite numerous summonses in public places, he had not surrendered himself.

Wignancourt, who was absent, wanted the embarrassing business over as quickly as possible, presumably according to his discreet instructions. Instead of discussing Caravaggio's assault on the distinguished knight, the assembly simply found him guilty of not giving himself up when summoned. A convenient clause in the statutes stated that any knight absent from the convent without written permission could be deprived of the habit, and expelled from the order.

In front of the oratory's altar, below Caravaggio's *Beheading of St. John,* stood a stool draped in a choir mantle, which represented Fra' Michelangelo. By a bitter irony, the worst humiliation of his life took place under a painting many consider his masterpiece. Having tried him in *absentia,* the assembly of the Religion condemned him to suffer the ultimate penalty, the much feared *Privatio Habitus,* or Loss of the Habit, and be "thrust forth like a rotten and putrid limb from our Order and Community." (This was the standard formula in such cases.) Finally, the black choir mantle with its white cross was symbolically ripped off the stool, as if ripping it off Fra' Michelangelo's shoulders.

Caravaggio always refused to accept the fact that he was no longer a Knight of Malta. He regarded his admission into the Religion as one of the supreme achievements of his life, placing him above all other painters. But, whatever he may have liked to think, his attempt to make a new beginning after Tommasoni's killing and his flight from Rome as an outlaw ended in irretrievable disaster and rejection. It severely damaged his chance of obtaining a papal pardon. No less alarmingly, it had involved him in a sinister vendetta with the unknown knight, though for the moment he was unaware of this. He was thirty-seven, entering middle age, and, for all his wonderful gifts, a hunted outcast. Despair might certainly help to account for some of his strange behavior in Sicily.

Syracuse, 1608–1609

The beautiful island of Sicily, technically part of the Kingdom of the Two Sicilies, was separated, administratively as well as geographically, from the mainland by the Straits of Messina, and ruled independently by a Spanish viceroy at Palermo. Caravaggio spent nearly a year on the island.

William Lithgow, who came in 1616, thought the Sicilians "generally wonderfull kind to strangers," if, among themselves, "ready to take revenge of any injury committed." He was astonished by the island's fertility; "the porest creature in Sicily eateth as good bread as the best Prince in Christendome doth." However, he warned that Sicily was far from safe, "ever sore oppressed with Rebells and Bandits." There was almost as much danger from the Barbary corsairs and the Turks; while Caravaggio was living on the island, the city of Reggio di Calabria, just across the Straits of Messina, was sacked by Turkish galleys. Lithgow cautioned against traveling along the coast, as Caravaggio would do often, because of the Moorish raiders who came at night and kidnapped the country people, "carrying them away captives to Barbary," despite the strong watchtowers.

We would know almost nothing about Caravaggio's visit to Sicily were it not for Francesco Susinno's manuscript history of the artists of his native city, Messina. If sometimes unreliable and padded out with details borrowed from Bellori, it contains information found in no other source. Clearly, both Caravaggio's genius and his aggressive eccentricity were long remembered by the Sicilians. Susinno must have had access to contemporary accounts of him, in letters or memoirs that perished in the earthquakes that destroyed Messina.

Understandably, Caravaggio was in a mood of black despair. "After leaving his profession [as a Knight], Caravaggio started to question a good deal about our most holy Religion, from which he gained the reputation of being a miscreant," Susinno tells us. By "Religion" he means the Order of Malta, not Christianity, as some historians have mistakenly supposed. He had forfeited what he regarded as his spiritual vocation and his social position. Nevertheless, he stubbornly continued to call himself a Knight of Malta, and presumably to wear the cross round his neck.

Susinno continues, "As a man, he was very distracted . . . caring little how he lived. . . . This was due to a mind scarcely less disturbed than the sea at Messina with its raging currents. . . . He always went armed, so that he looked more like an assassin than a painter." He also seems to have acquired another large black dog, a successor to Cornacchia, who performed similar tricks, accompanying his master everywhere. Susinno's considered opinion of Caravaggio was "a lunatic and quite crazy."

Syracuse was the most important Sicilian city after Palermo, renowned among antiquarians for its huge Roman amphitheater. In the quarries where the Athenian prisoners were confined after failing to capture the city in the fifth century B.C., there is a man-made, serpentine cavern, the *Orecchio di Dionigi,* or "Ear of Dyonisius," famous for its echoes, which legend says was carved out for the Sicilian tyrant Dyonisius. He is supposed to have hidden in the cavern, eavesdropping on the prisoners.

The legend, in reality, is a monumental joke, fabricated by Caravaggio, who had been taken to see the cavern by the celebrated archaeologist Vincenzo Mirabella. "Don't you see, in order to make an ear-trumpet for listening, the Tyrant used as his model what nature had used for the same purpose?" Caravaggio is credited with telling the credulous Mirabella. "So he made this cave just like an ear." Despite his misfortunes, he had not lost his sardonic humor.

On a rocky point of land between two havens, the city was dominated by the massive Castello Maniace, a Byzantine fortress rebuilt in the thirteenth century by the Hohenstauffen emperor Frederick II. In Caravaggio's time it housed the inevitable Spanish garrison. The threat from Muslim raiders was unrelenting. Every night, troops of horsemen had to ride out to search the seacoast for signs of danger. Nonetheless, amid its ruins, Syracuse was beautiful and opulent, a pleasant refuge for an exile. George Sandys remarked on the inhabitants' dignity, and on how the women's faces were hidden by their long black mantillas. If it was hot, there were plenty of gardens, watered by cooling springs.

Susinno informs us that when Caravaggio arrived at Syracuse he was given a warm welcome by an old friend from Roman days, Mario Minniti, who had returned to his native island and remarried after the death of his first wife. Minniti had become a well-established local painter, setting up a workshop at Syracuse. He welcomed Caravaggio "with all the kindness to be expected from such a gentleman." Susinno says that Minniti begged the Syracusan senate to offer Caravaggio a commission, partly because he wanted to keep his old friend in Syracuse for as long as possible, and partly because he hoped to learn as much as possible from him, since he had heard that Caravaggio "had become Italy's greatest painter."

The city's unusually likable patron saint was the charming St. Lucy, who had escorted Dante to the gate of Purgatory. The wealthy daughter of a Syracusan noble family, in the fourth century she had been denounced as a Christian by the man to whom she was betrothed, after giving away her entire fortune. Commanded by the consul Paschasius to sacrifice to the pagan gods, she staunchly refused. "Then Paschasius summoned panders and said to them, 'Invite the crowd to have their pleasure with this woman, and let them abuse her body till she dies,'" *The Golden Legend* relates. But the panders were unable to carry her off. Even oxen could not drag her away. "Then the consul, beside himself with rage, commanded that a great fire should be built around her, and that pitch, resin and boiling tar should be thrown on her. This, too, made no impression on the dauntless maiden. When a sword was plunged into her throat, she cried out that the Church had triumphed. 'This day Maximilian has died and Diocletian has been driven from the throne.'" As she spoke, officers came from Rome to seize Paschasius and put him to death. Lucy lived long enough for a priest to bring her Communion before she died.

Although there is no mention in *The Golden Legend* of St. Lucy being blinded by her tormentors, as is sometimes claimed, another legend relates how, when a besotted admirer praised the beauty of her eyes excessively, she tore them out and gave them to him on a plate, whereupon they were miraculously restored to her. The story probably derives from her name, which means "light." She was regarded as a saint who could cure any disease of the eyes. Blindness was commoner in the seventeenth century than it is now, and the church of Santa Lucia al Sepolcro, just outside Syracuse's walls, built where she is said to have been martyred, attracted pilgrims from all over Sicily.

The Syracusan Senate commissioned an altarpiece of St. Lucy from Caravaggio, who must have heard the many tales about her. In Susinno's words, his picture shows "the martyr's corpse lying on the ground while the Bishop comes to bury her, and two workmen, who are the main figures . . . are digging a grave in which to lay her." This conveys neither the painting's savagery nor its melancholy. A terrible wound in the throat was later made less obvious by the artist, perhaps in response to protests, Lucy being a much loved patron. Filled with sadness, the huge canvas is essentially a painting of mourners. There is grief even on the faces of the grave diggers.

Caravaggio must have realized that if St. Lucy's bones had vanished long ago from their shrine in the dimly lit chapel beneath the church, her bones' former resting place was still deeply venerated, which is why he concentrated on the burial rather than the saint. The brushwork is less careful than in his Roman, Neapolitan, or Maltese paintings, the colors are fewer, and there is less light. It is likely that he painted without models, working from memory; the face of an old woman bending over the body seems familiar from his days in Rome. Even so, Syracuse was delighted by the tribute to its beloved patron saint, which was immediately hung over the high altar of her church.

The applause at Syracuse did little to soothe the painter's misery. "Michele's disgrace would not leave him alone," writes Bellori, who claims that he was terrified. Just what was he afraid of? It cannot have been the Order of Malta, since during his time in Sicily he was always in cities where it was much in evidence. However, Susinno speaks of his being "pursued by his injured antagonist," apparently meaning the unknown knight he had fought before being put in the Birdcage. It is possible he had heard that his former confrere had recovered and was planning a revenge.

According to Susinno, "Michelangelo's disturbed brain, ever fond of wandering through the world, made him leave the house of his friend Minniti soon after. So he went to Messina." This was during the winter, at the end of 1608 or the beginning of 1609. Was he fleeing from the unknown knight's hired killers, was he merely restless, or had he had an invitation from the Messinese? Whatever his reasons for leaving Syracuse, when apparently he had every reason to stay, Messina was not all that easy to reach. Sandys, from personal experience, warned travelers who were contemplating a journey overland that they would almost certainly be robbed and murdered by the country people.

As for traveling by sea to Messina, Fernand Braudel reminds us of the hazards of the Mediterranean at the beginning of the seventeenth century. "Anyone sailing in the winter knew very well that he was at the complete mercy of the elements, that he had to be on the alert all the time, and that he had every chance of seeing the storm lanterns hoisted." The Sicilian coast was especially dangerous. Although small vessels like the feluccas used by Caravaggio hugged the shore, their crews were well aware that at this time of year a lethal gale could blow up at any moment. The Straits of Messina had a terrifying name; their shores were littered with shipwrecks. Yet Caravaggio took his chance and sailed. He must have had some very good reasons for leaving in such a hurry.

Messina, 1609

On the Straits of Messina, with their lethal currents, the city at which Caravaggio landed has been obliterated by earthquakes. In his time, it was a gleaming white port, set beneath snowcapped mountains and defended by three massive castles. These fortresses were so strong that the inhabitants never bothered to shut the city gates, "in derision of the Turks." Running in a semicircle around a sickle-shaped harbor, Messina must have looked magnificent from the sea as he sailed in on board his felucca.

Rich from trade and silk-weaving, with many banking houses, it was governed by a *Stratego*, appointed by the viceroy, together with a senate elected by less than a thousand citizens. Arrogant patricians of ancient family, proud of their city's semi-independent status, they insisted that Messina was the true capital of Sicily, not Palermo, and the viceroy had to spend half the year here. "The city is garnished with beautiful buildings, both publike and private. Venus, Neptune, Castor and Pollux had here their Temples; whose ruines are now the foundations of Christian Churches," noted George Sandys in 1611. "Throughout the City there are fountaines of fresh water," while "there standeth an high Lanterne, which by light in the night directeth such ships as are to enter these perilous streightes."

There was, of course, a dark side. "The Sicilians," says Sandys, "are a people greedy of honour, yet given to ease and delights; talkative, meddlesome, dissentious, jealous and revengefull." Messina was dangerous, even by the standards of the age. Sandys tells of constant housebreaking and robbery, "while in their private revenges, no night doth pass without a murder." Men were frequently kidnapped in the streets and held to ransom.

As a Sicilian, Francesco Susinno was irritated by the way the Messinese at once preferred Caravaggio to their own obscure painters. He adds, "Caravaggio's newly acquired fame and the natural friendliness of the Messinese, who are always ready to like strangers, together with the man's sheer quality, all combined to such an extent that they wanted him to stay and gave him commissions."

At Messina there was a wealthy Genoese from the vast network of Genoese banking families that reached as far south as Sicily. There is some speculation, but no firm evidence, that Giovanni Battista de Lazzari had links with Caravaggio's Genoese patrons at Rome. In December, he commissioned a *Raising of Lazarus* that Caravaggio delivered the following June.

"When certain rich gentlemen of the Lazzari family were building a chapel near the high altar of the church of the Crociferi fathers, they decided to commission a large picture from this artist, agreeing on a price of a thousand scudi," Susinno tells us. "The painter proposed the *Raising of Lazarus,* in allusion to their family name. The said gentlemen were delighted, giving him every facility . . . his picture begins by showing on the left-hand side the Savior, with the Apostles, turning round and summoning the dead if once very much alive Lazarus, whose spirit has long since left him, while in the middle two workmen are lifting a large stone. Lazarus's corpse is held up by another workman and seems to be on the verge of waking. Close to Lazarus's head are his two sisters, watching him about to wake as if they were stunned. Michelangelo has given the sisters' faces the most wonderful beauty."

Susinno was, however, shocked by what he had heard about the methods used by "this madman of a painter." To give Lazarus exactly the right air of realism, he had a decomposing corpse dug up and given to some workmen to hold for him while he painted it. Unable to bear the horrible smell, they dropped it. He immediately drew his dagger, threatening to stab them, so that they had to pick it up again. Bellori says mysteriously that someone in the picture is placing his hand over his nose, to ward off the stench coming from the corpse. Either Bellori had not seen the painting for himself or else the man holding his nose has somehow disappeared from view over the years.

Susinno tells us there was an earlier picture, which Caravaggio destroyed. The Lazzari family had given him permission to paint just as he pleased, allowing him to work in secret. When the first painting was exhibited, it caused general astonishment, and several Messinese art lovers made critical remarks. Caravaggio exploded with rage. "Impulsive as ever, Michelangelo pulled out the dagger he always wore at his side, giving a magnificent picture so many angry blows that it was quickly ripped to pieces. After venting his rage on the wretched painting, he felt much better and soothed the horrified gentlemen, telling them not to worry because he would soon produce another, more suited to their taste."

The Raising of Lazarus confirmed the people of Messina's good opinion of Caravaggio. They could see that he was indeed "working well." Accordingly, the Messinese senate paid him a thousand scudi to paint an *Adoration of the Shepherds* for the city's Capuchin church, Santa Maria degli Angeli. Although the church vanished long ago, the picture has survived and is still at Messina, in the Museo Nazionale. Susinno thought it his best painting. "This great work of art alone would make him remembered for centuries to come." He relates how "various princes" tried to get possession of it but were prevented by the Capuchin Fathers appealing to the Senate. "I can truthfully say that this work is unique and Caravaggio's most masterly painting," he wrote. Beautiful though it is, not everyone would agree with him. Certainly, the delicate young Virgin's contentment is most moving, as is the faith on the strong, simple faces of St. Joseph and the shepherds. The donkey is charming too. Yet there is a brooding anticipation of the Crucifixion, almost a sense of approaching death.

If Susinno praised Caravaggio's painting during his stay at Messina, he was horrified by his behavior. Referring to the artist's destruction of the first version of the *Raising of Lazarus,* Susinno comments, "This barbarous and bestial deed resulted from a jealous, intolerant nature. For the same reason, he became enraged whenever he heard Messinese artists being praised." It is only fair to Caravaggio to remember that all of them were undeniably mediocre. Susinno was particularly upset by Caravaggio's contempt for one of his own favorites, Catalano l'Antico, now totally forgotten outside Sicily. He records resentfully how Caravaggio, "in his usual sarcastic way," compared a picture by Filippo Paladino with some by Catalano in the basilica of Santa Maria di Gesù, observing scornfully, "This one's a real painting, the others are only a pack of cards."

Among Caravaggio's private commissions in Messina were two large half pictures of St. Jerome for a local nobleman, Count Adonnino. In August 1609, Niccolo di Giacomo recorded that he had ordered four scenes of the Passion of Our Lord from Caravaggio, that the artist had already delivered a *Christ Carrying the Cross*, and that he was expecting to receive the other three by the end of the month. "One could recall several more fine works, which I omit for the sake of brevity," says Susinno, referring to Caravaggio's Messinese period. All these pictures must have perished in the various natural disasters that later overwhelmed the city.

In the note recording his commission of the four scenes from the Passion, Niccolo di Giacomo refers to Caravaggio's disturbed mind, his "twisted brain." Plainly, he made an odd impression on the Messinese. In addition, he acquired a reputation for debauchery, or at least high living. "Since our painter had become so famous, he earned a great deal of money, which he wasted on gallantries and places of ill fame," Susinno records primly. He then tells a sad little tale. "One day, going into the church of the Madonna del Pilero with certain gentlemen, one of them came up very politely to offer him holy water. When asked why he did so, the gentleman answered that it absolved venial sins. 'No need of it for me, then,' replied Caravaggio, 'since all mine are mortal.' "

Caravaggio must have been a spectator in June when the image of the *Madonna della Lettera* was borne through the streets. She took her name from the famous letter she had sent to "all the Messinese," dated 3 June A.D. 42 and authenticated by the Jesuits as a copy of a genuine letter; the original had been destroyed "out of malice," presumably by someone from Palermo. Normally it was enshrined in the high altar of the duomo, though occasionally it was borrowed for casting out especially stubborn devils or for helping a distinguished lady through a difficult pregnancy.

He was here too for the greatest day in the city's calendar, the feast of the Virgin Mary's Assumption into Heaven on 15 August, when the Madonna was again borne through Messina, with even more splendor. Magistrates and patricians marched up and down the streets in her honor, followed by the garrison, to the music of drums and fifes, and then by priests and friars bearing relics. Finally came the *Madonna della Lettera* on an immense tower on wheels. As high as a house with several stories, the tower was dragged along by ropes pulled by hundreds of men; on one story were musicians, on the second a choir, and on the third "a tribe of singing patriarchs." At the summit a young girl held a beautiful child, who represented the Virgin's soul. The huge car was cheered by the crowds as it trundled past, cannon firing salutes. When it arrived at the cathedral, it was greeted by two statues of the city's legendary founders, Madre and Griffone.

Caravaggio might have continued at Messina for much longer. He was making all the money he needed, and it was a delightful little city. Before it was obliterated by a final earthquake, Augustus Hare wrote of "the exquisite glints of blue sea with white sails skimming across it, and a background of roseate Italian mountains, which may be seen down every steep street."

Since Caravaggio remained for several months, he was obviously not worried about being seized by the Knights. Yet the city was the Religion's headquarters in Sicily and main transit depot for supplies from Europe. His old friend the prior of Messina, Fra' Antonio Martelli, was here throughout his visit, having arrived in April 1608 and staying until September 1609. Fra' Giacomo Marchese, at whose house he had been a guest when he first went to Malta, was also there during 1609. Bellori writes mysteriously that while Caravaggio was on Sicily, "fear hunted him from place to place," but it cannot have been fear of the Order of Malta that made him leave Messina hurriedly at an unknown date, since he hoped that the Religion would eventually forgive him. When the *Raising of Lazarus* arrived at the church where it was to hang, the note recording its delivery described Caravaggio as "Knight of Jerusalem," as he still called himself.

According to Susinno, the artist left the city in 1609 because of a ridiculous incident in which he again lost his temper and used violence. "On feast days he would sometimes wander off in the company of a certain schoolmaster called Don Carlo Pepe, who often took his pupils to the arsenal to amuse them. Galleys were built there in those days . . . Michele went to watch the movements of the boys while they were playing, so as to find ideas for the figures [in his paintings]. But the schoolmaster began to worry about his motives and asked him just what he thought he was doing. The question so disgusted the painter that, to make quite certain that he did not lose his name for being a complete lunatic, he gave the man a wound in the head."

Clearly, Don Carlo had started to suspect that Caravaggio had sexual designs on his pupils. It is no less plain from Caravaggio's furious reaction that he was outraged by the insinuation, especially from a schoolmaster; in seventeenth-century Italy schoolmasters had a very unpleasant reputation for pederasty. Even so, it was no excuse for stabbing poor Don Carlo, and, in consequence, the artist had to leave Messina in a hurry.

An informed guess for the date of Caravaggio's hasty departure from the city would be in late summer rather than in early autumn. The feast day on which the unfortunate quarrel with Don Pepe took place is most likely to have been the Virgin's Assumption on 15 August, while Messina's very flourishing and well-attended trade fair would obviously have provided a fugitive artist with an excellent opportunity for escaping. Ships arrived from all over the Mediterranean; some years later, a visitor to the fair counted not less than sixty galleys in the harbor, which would, of course, have been accompanied by many more lesser craft, such as feluccas. They gave him an unusually good chance of leaving Messina discreetly, though for a few days he may have had to hide on board. The Messinese authorities did not have the manpower to search several hundred vessels.

If Caravaggio wanted to stay in Sicily, which seems not improbable in the absence of a pardon from Rome, the logical place for him to take refuge next was Palermo, Messina's rival. Sailing very soon after the end of the the Messinese fair, he would have arrived there just before or during the last week of August 1609.

XXXIII

Palermo, 1609

Frustratingly, there is even less detailed information about Caravaggio's visit to Palermo than there is about his time at Messina. We know for certain that he had left Sicily altogether by early October 1609. Bellori and Susinno both say he went to Palermo and painted pictures there. Until thirty years ago, one of these might still be seen in the Palermitan church for which he had been asked to paint it. Yet although the artist's stay was obviously very short, with his painter's eye it must have been quite long enough for him to realize why Palermo deserved the affectionate name of *La Felice*.

It lay at the edge of the Conca d'Oro, the "Golden Shell," a vast and staggeringly fertile garden of olive groves, vineyards, and orangeries beside the Mediterranean, on a wide bay bounded by a great mountain to the north and a wooded headland to the south. Its situation surpassed even that of Naples. By all accounts, it was among the most beautiful and exotic cities in seventeenth-century Europe. Its bizarre architecture, an amazing blend of Byzantine, Romanesque, Arab, and African, was now being joined by Baroque, while the vegetation was almost Egyptian, with palm trees, cotton trees, locust trees, sugar cane, and cacti.

Palermo was not only the crowning place of the kings of the Two Sicilies, but the island's historic capital and administrative center. The viceroy's palace was here, and the Sicilian parliament met in the city every three years. This was a period when Sicilian nobles were deserting their castles and moving into Palermo. In consequence, there was plenty of money circulating in the city, so that a famous artist like Caravaggio had every prospect of quickly finding valuable commissions.

Almost as soon as he arrived, he produced a large *Nativity* for the church of the Oratorian Compagnia di San Lorenzo. He must have worked with amazing speed, or completed an already almost finished canvas that he brought with him in response to a specific invitation. Once again, there is a distinctly somber atmosphere in what is a traditionally joyful scene, as if in sad contemplation of the coming sorrows of Christ's Passion. One suspects that it reflects the painter's own melancholy.

At the very end of September, or possibly the very beginning of October 1609, Caravaggio left Sicily for good. Bellori claims that, after painting the *Nativity,* Caravaggio did not feel safe about staying there any longer. But he appears to have exaggerated the artist's fears in saying that he had hurried panic-stricken through the island. Even so, it does look as though he received news at Palermo that terrified him.

Susinno tells us that Caravaggio "went back to Naples again, pursued by his injured antagonist." Apparently, by "injured antagonist," Susinno did not mean the unlucky schoolmaster whom the artist had assaulted at Messina but the unknown Knight of Justice with whom he had quarreled so disastrously on Malta. Presumably, the latter had by now recovered from the wounds inflicted during the duel and was reliably reported to be planning a revenge. One historian has suggested, as a reason for leaving, that "Palermo must have been less pleasant to visit than Messina: Spanish control was more evident, and life was dominated by the Inquisition." Spanish control would be no less in evidence at Caravaggio's next port of call, Naples, while there is not the slightest hint that he had reason at any stage of his career to fear investigation by the Inquisition, which dealt purely with deviations from

Catholic doctrine and was not interested in mere moral lapses such as dueling or murder. What little information we have indicates that he fled from Sicily in fear for his life.

Caravaggio must have had to return to Messina from Palermo, since it was the invariable point of embarcation for the crossing from Sicily to the mainland. If he made the crossing on board a merchant ship, he would have gone through the choppy waters of the Straits of Messina, then northward out to sea. Convoys of large, well-armed merchantmen were equipped to deal with any corsairs they might encounter. After four days, they would put in at Ischia, reaching Naples the next day. But because Caravaggio was on the run, he presumably wanted to travel as unobtrusively as possible, so it is much more likely that he hired a felucca. If the crew noticed their passenger's queer bundles of rolled-up canvas, they could not possibly have guessed that they were valuable.

Since a felucca was too small to risk meeting a corsair, she had to sail by a different route after leaving the Straits of Messina, always keeping as close to the coast as possible. This was far slower than the direct route taken by the big ships, but it was much safer. It is unlikely to have been a comfortable voyage. Being at the end of September at earliest, stormy weather had probably begun to set in, so that it must have been well over a week before Caravaggio's felucca reached Naples, perhaps even as long as a fortnight. During the last twelve months, the artist had made four sea voyages. Like Odysseus, he had passed between Scylla and Carybdis on more than one occasion. The symbolism may seem oddly fitting for someone whose life was quite so stormy. But, unlike for Odysseus, there was to be no happy ending for Caravaggio.

XXXIV

"The Neapolitan Shrug," 1609

Even today, there are few pleasanter places to approach from the sea than Naples, passing between Capri and Ischia. Perhaps the beautiful prospect raised Caravaggio's spirits for a moment, but when he landed reality would soon catch up with him. Meanwhile, it seems that he went to stay at the Marchesa di Caravaggio's palace on the Riviera di Chiaia.

It was fear for his life that had brought him back to Naples. He was running from an implacable pursuer who, he must have known, was planning either to kill him or arrange for his death. Probably very few people were aware of the artist's arrival in the city, and he would have been perfectly safe so long as he stayed inside the marchesa's palace. Unfortunately, he was unable to resist the lure of the fleshpots. The famous tavern Osteria del Cirigio beckoned irresistibly, with its delicious food and wine, uproarious good company, and "free-living ladies." He must have known that the place was very dangerous, and that he would almost certainly be seen there by any enemy who was searching for him, but he took the risk.

Murders occurred in Naples every day, frequently committed by the upper classes. There seems to have been a positive mania for feuding and dueling among the haughty, hot-tempered, revengeful nobility of the southern kingdom, and Knights of Malta were often all too prominent in countless bloodthirsty confrontations in the city's narrow, dimly lit streets. At the same time, assassination was a highly efficient business, a murder being very easily and cheaply arranged, the famous "Neapolitan Shrug." Its extremely sinister practitioners had a terrifying reputation throughout Europe, which was obviously well deserved; an English secret agent credited them with poisoning their victims by envenoming the scent of flowers, strangling them with a fragment of fine linen thrust down their throats, piercing their windpipes with a needle point, or pouring mercury into their mouths as they slept. Generally, however, the sword or the knife was used. It is clear that there was never any difficulty in finding such men.

Caravaggio was about to fall victim to a relentless vendetta on the part of the Knight of Justice he had wounded so badly on Malta. There would be a deliberate, well-organized attempt to murder him. Probably the unknown knight was not personally involved in the actual attack. Since he had already been worsted in combat by Caravaggio, he can have had no wish to face him again at the point of a sword, and in any case he regarded him as a social inferior. It is therefore more than likely that he hired professional *bravi* to do the killing for him.

On 24 October 1609, an *avviso* sent to Urbino reported, "We learn from Naples that the celebrated painter Caravaggio has been killed, though others say only wounded." Bellori goes into more detail, recording how "he was stopped one day in the doorway of the Osteria del Ciriglio and surrounded by armed men, who attacked him and wounded him in the face." Baglione tells the same story, adding that the sword cuts on his face were so deep that he was almost unrecognizable. He was very lucky to escape with his life, being no doubt mistakenly left for dead.

He must have been dangerously ill for a long time. According to Bellori, he had not recovered from his wounds by the following July. Too weak to move, he could not leave where he was hiding, presumably in the marchesa's palace. During his convalescence, there was no mention of him in the Neapolitan police records, or in the Roman *avvisi,* which regularly reported gossip from Naples. He was in no condition for brawling. However, a single document shows that at some moment before May 1610 he had started painting again and was ready to accept commissions.

His last paintings are obsessively gloomy. He does not seem to have used models, perhaps because of his need to remain in hiding. It is unlikely that he could have produced all the pictures attributed to him during this second stay in Naples, although he may have sold some he had brought with him from Sicily, or even Malta. Perhaps he thought the Neapolitan nobles could afford to pay more than the Sicilian nobles. That his paintings were carried around may explain why so many have been mistaken for copies; rolling up the canvases made the paint flake, so that they had to be retouched.

Bellori writes of at least one picture painted during this second stay in Naples: "And hoping to placate the Grand Master, he sent him as a gift a half-figure of Herodias with the head of St. John in a basin." Perhaps it was accompanied by a plea for Fra' Alof to call off the unknown knight. Sir Denis Mahon believes that this painting was begun by Caravaggio immediately after his arrival in Naples but had to be put aside after the attempted murder at the Osteria del Ciriglio. Caravaggio never stopped hoping for a pardon from the Religion, continuing to call himself a Knight of Malta until the day he died.

When Caravaggio took refuge in Genoa in 1605, after attacking Pasqualone, he had declined to paint a fresco for Marcantonio Doria, the son of a former Doge. On 11 May 1609, Lanfranco Massa, the Doria family's agent at Naples, wrote a letter to Prince Marcantonio, saying that soon he would be able to send a painting by Caravaggio to Genoa. This was the *Martyrdom of St. Ursula.* Massa explained that he was having to wait because the artist had applied the varnish so thickly; Massa had left the picture to dry in the sun, with disastrous consequences—it had had to be revarnished.

(In the same letter, Massa refers to Caravaggio as Marcantonio's "friend," implying that they had met fairly frequently, no doubt in Rome.) The painting finally left Naples for Genoa on May 17.

It was probably commissioned by Marcantonio Doria for the convent of his beloved stepdaughter, Sister Orsola. The story of the gruesome martyrdom that it depicts comes from *The Golden Legend,* which tells how the virgin Ursula was murdered by a king of the Huns for refusing to marry him, and how he shot her with an arrow. The king is a gnome-like figure in a Baroque cuirass, grimly clutching an oriental bow, while an impassive Ursula gazes with strange calm at the arrow in her bosom that has killed her.

Cruelty of a different sort is in *The Tooth-Drawer,* a rare exception from Caravaggio's usual religious themes. A 1637 inventory of paintings at the Palazzo Pitti in Florence lists such a picture, while in his *Microcosmo della Pittura,* published twenty years after the inventory, Francesco Scannelli relates how he saw in the grand duke of Tuscany's apartments "a painting of half-length figures with [Caravaggio's] accustomed naturalism." Scannelli adds that it was in very bad condition. *The Tooth-Drawer*'s authenticity has been accepted only in recent years, and not by everybody. Dating from the artist's second stay at Naples, it is notable for the grotesque spectators' fascinated enjoyment of the patient's agony.

The *Denial of St. Peter* also dates from this second Neapolitan period, inspired by the Gospel of St. Mark: "Now when Peter was in the court below, there cometh one of the maidservants of the high priest. And when she had seen Peter warming himself, looking on him, she saith: 'Thou also wast with Jesus of Nazareth.' But he denied, saying: 'I neither know nor understand what thou sayest.' " An uneasy St. Peter and the suspicious maidservant have their faces illuminated by the firelight behind them, heightening the chiaroscuro, while a bystander's face remains wholly in shadow.

Another *David and Goliath* shows a handsome young David holding up an agonized head, which, however, wears a curiously reflective expression.

Once again, it is a self-portrait. David holds a broad-bladed "sword-rapier" of the type that may have slashed Caravaggio's face at the Osteria del Ciriglio. The picture has also been attributed to his second Neapolitan period. A tent flap at the top left-hand corner indicates that the scene is not the moment immediately after David killed Goliath, but another, described in the Book of Kings: "And when David was returned after the Philistine was slain, Abner took him in before Saul with the head of the Philistine in his hand." No one can be unmoved by this painting.

Some think that this interpretation of *David and Goliath* is meant to convey the artist's foreboding of imminent death, since Goliath appears to see something we cannot. Both faces are self-portraits, Goliath being the middle-aged, sinful Caravaggio, while David is Caravaggio restored to his youthful innocence. The most likely meaning is that the painter is showing the pure, intelligent soul freed from the battered, sinful body, released from suffering and grief, redeemed by Christ. This is probably how most contemporaries familiar with alchemy would have read it. The picture was acquired by Cardinal Borghese, who remained one of Caravaggio's greatest admirers.

Another work, ascribed to the same period, although it may have been produced in Sicily, is an *Annunciation.* One of Caravaggio's most mysterious and saddest paintings, it was his last altarpiece, commissiond by Duke Henry II of Lorraine for the high altar of the cathedral at Nancy. Inspired by the Gospel of St. Luke, it shows a strapping, winged angel hovering over a submissive, abject Virgin, as he brings his wonderful message to her: "And Mary said: 'Behold the handmaid of the Lord: be it done to me according to thy word.' " What is striking is the Virgin's haunted desolation, her look of utter dejection at the prospect of giving birth to the Messiah. The desolation may well reflect Caravaggio's own wretchedness. If the *Annunciation* was painted in Naples, and not in Sicily, then the bed and the chair at the right of Mary's chamber could be those of the artist's sickroom.

During 1609–1610, his normal gloom must have been intensified by terrifying memories of the attempt to kill him, the constant pain of slowly healing wounds, and the frustrations of an invalid's life. His brooding, melancholy temperament made him peculiarly ill-equipped to bear such miseries. Yet, when examined objectively, his future still seemed glowing.

As early as 1606, there had been rumors in Rome of a pardon. In May 1607, and again in August the same year, the Duke of Modena's Roman agent reported that efforts were being made to secure one. During the first months of 1610, Cardinal Ferdinando Gonzaga, who now owned the *Death of the Virgin,* begged Pope Paul to forgive the artist. Vain and weak, Gonzaga was scarcely a papal favorite, but almost certainly he was warmly supported by Cardinal Scipione Borghese, who wanted his favorite painter back in Rome. For Caravaggio, a pardon meant not only returning to Rome but a guarantee that he would be feted as the greatest artist of the age. He could command an enormous income, and powerful friends in the College of Cardinals might even persuade the pope to restore the habit to "Fra' Michelangelo."

Meanwhile, he appears to have gone on working despite his poor health. Although the one surviving picture that can be dated with absolute certainty to this Neapolitan period is the *Martyrdom of St. Ursula,* the fact that he was able to paint it shows that he was regaining his strength. Probably he seldom left the marchesa's palace, let alone dared to visit the Ciriglio. He seems, however, to have gone to the Lombard community's church of Sant' Anna dei Lombardi, painting two pictures for the Fenarolli Chapel. One was a *St. Francis Receiving the Stigmata,* the other a *Resurrection of Christ,* considered by some to be excessively naturalistic because, instead of depicting Christ in glory, the artist showed him with one foot still inside the grave. Both were destroyed by an earthquake in 1793.

Naples was the ideal place to wait for news of his pardon, since it was so close to the Papal States and a mail coach regularly brought letters from Rome. Nevertheless, by midsummer 1610 Caravaggio had become desperately anxious to get out of the city. He may have heard from friends that the unknown knight had learned he was still alive and in Naples and was planning another attempt to murder him.

Some historians suggest that Caravaggio left Naples on a boat bound for Genoa. But of his principal Genoese friends, the Giustiniani brothers and Ottavio Costa lived in Rome, while he could easily do business with Prince Doria without visiting Genoa. Rome had far more to offer him. Baglione and Bellori both say his destination was Rome. The only difference between their accounts is that Baglione thought Cardinal Gonzaga was still negotiating with Rome for the pardon, while Bellori thought he had already obtained it. There is also evidence that the cardinal secretary knew Caravaggio was on his way to Rome, bringing pictures with him, though he did not know how many or what they were. Obviously, these were intended for Borghese and Gonzaga, perhaps even for the pope himself. It looks as if Scipione Borghese had received a letter, either from the marchesa or from the artist, before Caravaggio left Naples.

According to Bellori, Caravaggio, "despite suffering agonizing pain, went on board a felucca as soon as possible with his few possessions, and set off for Rome." This was early in July. Probably he fancied that, from his hostess's window, he could see his enemy's *bravi* lurking outside. A recently discovered report from the nuncio in Naples, Bishop Deodato Gentile, sent to Borghese at the end of July, says that he left "from the house of the Signora Marchesa di Caravaggio di Caravaggio, who lives on the Chiaia." The felucca would have anchored just off the seafront, immediately below her palace, so that he could go aboard and embark without attracting too much attention.

XXXV

"Puerto Hercules," July 1610

Porto Ercole was close to the northern border of the Papal States, not far from Civitavecchia. Today a seaside resort, in the seventeenth century it was a Spanish garrison town, one of the *presidie,* a string of enclaves on the Tuscan coast from which Spain monitored shipping between France and Naples. Its only other activities were fishing and the grain trade. The Spaniards called the little port *Puerto Hercules*. Probably Caravaggio had never even heard of it before now.

The skipper of his felucca must have intended to sail slowly along the coast in the usual way, landing every evening to spend the night within reach of a fort. But, almost as soon as they had left Naples, a storm came up. People on shore thought the felucca might have run for shelter to the island of Procida, off the direct sea route, though only two miles out from Naples, which explains why a rumor later circulated that Caravaggio had died on the island. In reality, the gale blew the tiny ship northward and past Ostia, the landing place for Rome. At last the skipper managed to put in to Palo, still in papal territory, a fishing hamlet guarded by a fort with a small garrison.

Unfortunately, the Spanish captain at the fort had just been warned to be on the lookout for a well-known bandit. Seeing a pugnacious little man in shabby finery, armed with rapier and dagger, his face scarred by sword cuts, the captain at once assumed that Caravaggio was the *banditto*. "When he landed on the beach, he was arrested in error and imprisoned for two days," says Baglione. Bellori confirms that the soldiers in the fort had been waiting for "another gentleman," obviously the bandit. The mistake gives some idea of the impression Caravaggio made on anyone meeting him for the first time. The nuncio adds that he had to pay the captain a large sum of money before he would let him go. Baglione and Bellori both thought that the arrest occurred at Porto Ercole. Only since the discovery of the nuncio's report has it been known that it took place at Palo. On the whole, however, they seem to be reasonably accurate, while the nuncio supplies vital details.

When Caravaggio was released, his felucca was nowhere to be seen, which sent him into a frenzy. His possessions were still on board, including his paintings. He ran along the beach like a lunatic, searching for the boat, until told that she had been blown even farther north. Learning she was at Porto Ercole, he hurried after her. Since most of his money had been stolen from him by the captain, he could not afford to hire another felucca and was forced to travel a hundred kilometers overland from Palo, possibly on foot, despite the risk of being murdered by peasants or *banditti*. He may have had enough funds left to hire a horse or a mule, but in the heat of the July sun, even if he rode, it would have been a grueling journey.

Already faint from painful, unhealed wounds, further weakened by his ordeal at sea and his imprisonment, and worn out by his trek from Palo, Caravaggio was exhausted and half crazy by the time he arrived at Porto Ercole. He rushed off to look for the felucca and his pictures, but soon collapsed. Baglione tells us that "he reached a place on the seashore where he was put to bed with a deadly fever, and after a few days he died miserably, with no one to care for him." The "place" [*luogo*] sounds like a boathouse or a shed for nets. Mancini, too, says, "he died in want, and without treatment." Caravaggio's death was 18 July 1610. He was thirty-eight years old.

In 1995 Professor Maurizio Marini discovered a document in the archives of the local diocese that shed fresh light on the painter's death and burial. He died from drinking polluted water, contracting some lethal form of enteric fever. He did not die alone as Baglione and Mancini thought, but was nursed by the Confraternity of Santa Cruz. Its members, officers of the Spanish garrison at Porto Ercole, saw that dying wayfarers received medicine and the Sacraments, took inventories of their goods, and, when possible, sent their bodies home for reburial. They owned the little chapel of St. Sebastian near the sea, next to Fort Filippo, which had a small garden with two palm trees. They interred him here, between the palm trees. Despite the fact that it was a pauper's burial, it is unlikely that the confraternity robbed his corpse. The chapel is still standing, no longer a place of worship, and although his grave has not yet been found, Caravaggio must lie nearby, rapier and dagger by his side, wearing his cross and wrapped in a knight's choir mantle, the shroud of every Knight of Malta.

Recently, it has been unconvincingly suggested that the traditional account of Caravaggio's death was an official fabrication by the knights and the local authorities to conceal his murder, which, supposedly, had taken place in a dungeon at Civitavecchia in papal territory with the connivance of the Catholic Church. It is alleged that the Knights of Malta had never forgiven him for the mysterious crime he had committed at Valletta in 1608, whose details they suppressed for reasons unknown. Yet not only had their grand master helped the painter to escape from Malta, but, had they wanted to, the knights could easily have arranged for him to be murdered while he was in Sicily. It seems unlikely that they would have risked infuriating Cardinal Borghese by killing one of his favorite artists, whose pardon he had only just obtained from the pope with great difficulty. And there is no known record of the Religion murdering anybody in such a way throughout its entire history.

Certainly, no one could have been more taken aback by the unexpected news of Caravaggio's death than Scipione Borghese, who was aghast at the loss of his eagerly awaited paintings. He immediately sent orders for the nuncio at Naples to find out exactly what had happened, in particular what had happened to his pictures. In the report, dated 29 July, the obsequious Bishop Gentile was careful to refer to the artist as *il povero Caravaggio*. He knew very well that he was writing about a favorite. He describes Caravaggio's last journey in detail, mentioning the mistaken rumor that he had died on Procida. Then he deals with the paintings. "The felucca, when it got back, brought his belongings to the house of the Signora Marchesa di Caravaggio," he states. "I at once went to look for the pictures, but found they were no longer there, except for three, two of St. John and one of the Magdalene, and these are at the Signora Marchesa's house." In fact, the three were the only pictures that had been on board the felucca. Borghese was determined to get possession of them.

From a copy of a document prepared by officials of the viceroy of Naples, which was destroyed during the Second World War, it seems that the inventory of Caravaggio's effects drawn up by the Confraternity of Santa Cruz was sent to the Religion at Valletta. The Knights of Malta, however, refusing to acknowledge him as a member of their order, declined to accept even the pictures. The viceroy then ordered that all of Caravaggio's possessions be sent to the Viceregal Palace, "especially the painting of St. John the Baptist." But Cardinal Borghese prevailed. *St. John the Baptist in the Wilderness* is still in his collection at the Villa Borghese.

On July 28, the duke of Urbino's agent in Rome sent his employer an *avviso* reporting, "News has arrived of the death of Michel Angelo Caravaggio, the celebrated artist, most excellent as a colorist and in imitating nature, after his illness at Porto Ercole." On August 1, another *avviso* informed its readers that "Michel Angelo da Caravaggio, the famous painter, has died at Porto Ercole when traveling from Naples to Rome, thanks to the mercy of His Holiness in canceling a warrant for murder."

Bellori relates how everyone in Rome had been waiting for Caravaggio to return, telling us, with perhaps a little exaggeration, that the news of his death "caused universal sorrow." But Sandrart was undoubtedly echoing the Giustiniani brothers and their circle when he wrote, "His passing was mourned by all the leading noblemen in Rome, because one day he might have done so much more for art." Years later, his rakish old friend, the Cavaliere Marino, whose portrait he had once painted, published some affectionate verses in his memory, "In morte di Michelangelo da Caravaggio":

There has been a cruel plot against you,
Michele, by Death and by Nature . . .

The Cavaliere claimed that Caravaggio had not merely painted, he had created.

An unforgiving Baglione wrote with relish that Caravaggio "died badly, just as he had lived." It is only fair to remember that more than a few artists of the Baroque age possessed difficult temperaments, were no less violent, and had even stormier careers, yet in the end they generally settled down. An increasingly held view in seventeenth-century Italy was that most, if perhaps not all, artists and creative writers were slightly mad. Pope Paul V is credited with observing, "Everything is permitted to painters and poets: we have to put up with these great men because the superabundance of spirits that makes them great is the same that leads to such strange behavior."

Although Caravaggio's earliest paintings had secular themes, he was primarily a religious artist. Essentially he was a man who, when painting, became a mystic. His deepest affliction was not his violent temper but a devouring melancholy. Yet despite his misfortunes and his early death, he should not be seen as a tragic figure. Nor would he have seen himself as one. The last version of *David and Goliath* was inspired by his conviction that, ultimately, he would triumph over sin and death, escaping from the unhappy man he had become. Caravaggio's portrait of his own severed head, grasped by his redeemed self, was a declaration of hope.

EPILOGUE

Caravaggio's reputation continued to grow steadily, and so many painters tried to copy his style that art historians speak of "Caravaggists." It was only to be expected that his pictures found a place in the collections of Charles I of England and Louis XIV of France. In 1750, Pope Clement XIV presented a *St. John* to the new Capitoline Museum at Rome. In 1780, during the dissolution of the Flemish monasteries, Emperor Joseph II confiscated the *Madonna of the Rosary* from the Dominicans and added it to the imperial collection in Vienna.

Many people have always been of two minds about Caravaggio. Berenson may seem eccentric in arguing that he was not a Baroque artist, yet at the height of the Baroque there were reservations about Caravaggio. Mancini criticized his "school" for a frequent "lack of movement, expression and elegance." Baglione admitted that his style was beautiful, but thought he had "poor judgement in selecting what was good and leaving out what was bad." Bellori admired many of his pictures, particularly those in his early style, but was horrified by what he regarded as his coarse naturalism, his concentration on "common, vulgar things." Poussin went even further, saying that Caravaggio "had come into the world to destroy painting." However, for many years hostile critics like this were in a minority, and he remained among Europe's acknowledged great masters.

In 1764, in an *Essay on Painting*, the Venetian savant Francesco Algarotti could still call Caravaggio "The Rembrandt of Italy," alluding to "the magic of his chiaroscuro." But, in the age of the rococo and then of the neoclassical, he was going out of favor. At about the time Algarotti wrote, the German artist Anton Rafael Mengs claimed, "Caravaggio possessed neither variety nor moderation, so that in consequence his draftmanship was very inferior." It was an amazing statement, but the fact that Mengs, the king of Spain's court painter, was able to make it shows just how much popular taste had turned against Caravaggio. In 1789 a highly respected historian of Italian art, Luigi Lanzi, sneered that Caravaggio's men and women were "memorable only for their vulgarity . . . and lived in dungeons."

Writing during the 1850s, the great Swiss historian Jacob Burckhardt could refer dismissively to "the crude style of Caravaggio." In England, the Victorians were especially hostile. John Ruskin, for example, found Caravaggio neither great nor sincere, solemnly placing him "among worshippers of the depraved." John Addington Symonds compared Caravaggio's paintings with the novels of Zola, blaming him not only for "vulgarity" but for "a crude realism," grumbling, "it seems difficult for realism, either in literature or art, not to fasten upon ugliness, vice, pain and disease, as though these imperfections of our nature were more real than beauty, goodness, pleasure and health."

By the early years of the twentieth century, however, the cultivated were once more beginning to appreciate Caravaggio. In 1905, Roger Fry declared that he was "in many senses the first modern artist . . . the first to rely entirely on his own temperamental aptitude and to defy tradition and authority." Dedicated scholars, notably Roberto Longhi, started looking for his paintings and, in consequence, the number of works attributed to him has more than doubled, even if several attributions may not be universally accepted. Some have been tracked down after disappearing during the long years of disfavor, while others previously thought to be copies have been recognized as originals. The *Bacchino Malato* and even the *Judith and Holofernes* were found only during the late 1940s. Since then, Mina Gregori has discovered the portrait of a Knight of Malta, recently identified as Fra' Antonio Martelli. More exciting still has been the finding of *The Cardsharps* and *The Taking of Christ*. It is far from impossible that other paintings still await rediscovery. One reason for their disappearance may be that, when his white or cream tones go yellow with age, all the light leaves his canvases, though this returns miraculously with modern techniques of restoration.

There have also been some tragic losses, such as the pictures that perished during the Russian army's capture of Berlin in 1945, the portrait of *The Courtesan Fillide,* and the first version of the *Inspiration of St. Matthew*. The *Nativity with St. Francis and St. Lawrence*, stolen in 1969, may never be recovered. In 1984, the *St. Jerome* was stolen from St. John's church at Valletta. Thanks, however, to the patient negotiations of the Maltese Director of Museums, Marius Zerafa, and his advice to the police, it was recovered in 1987. Some suspect that, as in the case of the Palermo *Nativity,* the Mafia were involved in the theft.

So much attention is devoted by scholars to Caravaggio's art and to his mysterious life that it has been called the Caravaggio industry. It is, undeniably, a very productive industry. If it is not quite true to say that new discoveries are made every year, we certainly know more about him than we did two decades ago. For example, during the 1970s Mia Cinotti published the Roman police reports with the details of his nightlife, while during the 1980s other historians revealed the Marchesa di Caravaggio's unsuspected role, the unsavory reputation of Captain Ranuccio Tommasoni, and the papal dispensation that enabled Caravaggio to become a Knight of Malta. One day they may even be able to tell us the identity of his enemy, the unknown knight, and the real reason he was put in the Birdcage.

Caravaggio fascinates, and not only because of his wonderful pictures. It is thirty years since Kenneth Clark described him as "like the hero of a modern play," meaning, of course, an antihero. He had all the qualities needed for the part. A portrait drawing of him by Ottavio Leoni looks very like the face of a certain type of modern antihero, sulky and resentful, with puzzled, unreliable eyes and a sneering mouth. However anachronistic, this resemblance to an antihero may perhaps explain why he casts so powerful a spell at the end of the twentieth century.

APPENDIX:

WHERE TO SEE CARAVAGGIO'S PICTURES

Caravaggio is exceptional among great artists of his period in that so many of his works can be seen in the churches or palaces for which he painted them. A comprehensive list of his pictures, and of others attributed to him with varying degrees of plausibility, is A. O. della Chiesa, L'Opera completa del Caravaggio *(Milan, 1981), but for obvious reasons it needs updating. The following are Caravaggio's most important paintings. It should be remembered that they are sometimes removed for restoration or on loan to exhibitions.*

Italy

ROME

San Luigi dei Francesi (Contarelli Chapel): *Calling of St. Matthew, Martyrdom of St. Matthew,* and *Inspiration of St. Matthew (St. Matthew and the Angel)*

Santa Maria del Popolo (Cerasi Chapel): *Conversion of St. Paul* and *Crucifixion of St. Peter*

Sant' Agostino: *Madonna di Loreto*

Palazzo Barberini: *Judith and Holofernes* and *St. John the Baptist*

Galleria Borghese: *David and Goliath, Madonna dei Palafrenieri, St. Jerome, St. John the Baptist, Boy with a Basket of Fruit,* and *Bacchino Malato*

Galleria Doria Pamphili: *Rest on the Flight into Egypt, Mary Magdalene,* and *St. John the Baptist*

Odescalchi Collection: *Conversion of St. Paul*

Palazzo Corsini: *Narcissus*

Pinacoteca Capitolina: *Il Pastor Friso*

Vatican Gallery: *Entombment of Christ*

FLORENCE

Uffizi: *Bacchus, Head of Medusa,* and *Sacrifice of Isaac*

Palazzo Pitti: *Sleeping Cupid* and *Portrait of a Knight of Malta*

MILAN

Pinacoteca di Brera: *Supper at Emmaus*

Pinacoteca Ambrosiana: *Basket of Fruit*

NAPLES

Palace of Capodimonte: *Seven Works of Mercy* and *Flagellation*

Banco Commerciale: *Martyrdom of St. Ursula*

Sicily

MESSINA

Museo Nazionale: *Resurrection of Lazarus* and *Adoration of the Shepherds*

SYRACUSE

Church of Santa Lucia: *Burial of St. Lucy*

Austria

VIENNA

Kunsthistorisches Museum: *Madonna of the Rosary*

Britain

LONDON

National Gallery: *Supper at Emmaus, Salome with the Head of St. John the Baptist,* and *Boy Bitten by a Lizard*

France

PARIS

Louvre: *Death of the Virgin* and *Grand Master Alof de Wignancourt*

Germany

BERLIN

Gemäldegalerie: *Amor Vincit Omnia*

Ireland

DUBLIN

National Gallery of Ireland: *Taking of Christ*

Malta

VALLETTA

Church of St. John: *Beheading of St. John the Baptist* and *St. Jerome*

Spain

MADRID

Prado: *Salome with the Head of St. John the Baptist*

Thyssen-Bornemisza Collection: *St. Catherine*

United States

NEW YORK

Metropolitan Museum: *Concert of Musicians* and *Denial of St. Peter*

CLEVELAND

Cleveland Museum of Art: *Crucifixion of St. Andrew*

DETROIT

Detroit Institute of Arts: *Conversion of the Magdalene*

FORT WORTH

Kimball Arts Museum: *Cardsharps*

HARTFORD

Wadsworth Atheneum: *Ecstasy of St. Francis*

KANSAS CITY

Nelson Gallery: *St. John the Baptist*

Throughout Europe and the United States there are other paintings said to be Caravaggios. Some may be genuine.

The main contemporary, or near contemporary, sources are:

Baglione, G. *Le vite de' pittori, scultori et architetti . . .* Rome, 1642. Facsimile, ed. V. Mariani, Rome, 1935.

Bellori, P. *Le vite de' pittori, scultori e architetti moderni*. Rome, 1672. Ed. E. Borea, Turin, 1976.

Mancini, G. *Considerazioni sulla pittura . . .* Rome, c. 1617–1630. Ed. A. Marucchi & L. Salerno, Rome, 1956–1957.

Mander, K. van. *Het Schilder-boek*. Haarlem, 1604.

Sandrart, J. von. *Academie der Bau, Bild, und Mahlerey-Künste von 1675*. Ed. A. R. Peltzer, Munich, 1925.

Susinno, F. *Le vite di' pittori messinesi . . .* Ed. V. Martinelli, Florence, 1960.

No satisfactory English translations exist of any of these works, while, although useful, the English versions of key extracts given in Howard Hibbard's *Caravaggio* (New York, 1983) are not invariably reliable.

The following notes refer to material other than the main sources.

PAGES

ix "*with none for decent living*." Bernard Berenson, *Del Caravaggio: delle sue incongruenze e della sua fama*. Florence, 1951 (translated as *Caravaggio: His Incongruity and His Fame*, New York, 1953).

1 *his brother Giovan Battista*. M. Calvesi, *La realtà del Caravaggio*. Turin, 1990.

1 Mancini, *Considerazioni sulla pittura*.

2 *Just over forty kilometers*. R. Ziglioli, *Il Caravaggio . . . a Caravaggio, in Roma*, in *Michelangelo Merisi da Caravaggio: La vita e le opere attraverso i documenti* (ed. S. Macioce), Rome [1997].

3 *"the garden of Italy."* Thomas Coryate, *Coryate's Crudités*. London, 1611.

3 *"level Lombardy."* Henry James, *Italian Hours*. London, 1909.

3 *Fermo's duties*. F. Liberati, *Il Perfetto Maestro di Casa*. Rome, 1658.

4 *his wife, Donna Costanza Colonna*. Calvesi, *La realtà del Caravaggio*.

4 *"Milan is a sweet place." Diary of John Evelyn*. London, 1955.

6 *Borromeo*. E. Ginex Palmieri, *San Carlo. L'uomo e la sua epoca*. Milan, 1984.

10 *His master*. E. Baccheschi, *"Simone Peterzano,"* in *I Pittori bergameschi dal XIII al XIX secolo. Il Cinquecento*. Bergamo, 1978.

11 *Brescia, Cremona, Lodi, and Bergamo*. M. Cinotti, "*La Giovinezza del Caravaggio. Ricerche e scoperte*," in *Novità sul Caravaggio*. Milan, 1975.

13 *"The black mummified corpse*." Henry James, *Italian Hours*.

14 *The fathers of the council*. E. Male, *L'Art réligieux après le Concile du Trente*. Paris, 1932.

15 *What gave the council's decrees such force*. H. O. Evenett, *The Spirit of the Counter Reformation*. Cambridge, 1968.

17 *why Caravaggio left Milan*. Calvesi, *La realtà del Caravaggio.*

18 *Milanese rapiers were famous*. E. Valentine, *Rapiers*. London, 1968.

18 *botta lunga*. E. Castle, *Schools and Masters of Fencing*. London, 1892.

20 "*nothing but a sepulchre*." M. de Montaigne, *Journal de Voyage*. Paris, 1906.

21 "*shewed us all the monuments*." Thomas Nashe, *The Unfortunate Traveller*. London, 1594.

25 *only recently elected*. L. von Pastor, *The History of the Popes*, vol. 23, *Clement VIII (1592–1605),* London, 1933.

27 *The Oratorians*. C. Ponelle and L. Bordet, *Saint Philippe Neri et la société romaine de son temps*. Paris, 1929.

32 *a French picture dealer*. The dealer may not have been Valentin but Costantino Spata, whose shop was next door. S. Corradino and M. Marini, "The Earliest Account of Caravaggio in Rome," *The Burlington Magazine,* January 1998.

34 *something of an enigma*. Z. Waźbiński, *Il cardinale Francesco Maria del Monte (1549–1626). Mecenate di artistici, consigliere di politici e di sovrani*. Florence, 1994.

34 *Chacon's massive history*. A. Chacon, A. Oidoino et al., *Vitae et res gestis pontificum et SRE cardinalium*. Rome, 1677.

36 *his complex, subtle patron*. F. Haskell, *Patrons and Painters*. London, 1980.

36 *Examination of Ameyden's* avvisi. C. Gilbert, *Caravaggio and His Two Cardinals*. University Park, Pa., 1995.

37 *a taste for girls*. L. Spezzaferro, "*La cultura del cardinale del Monte e il primo tempo del Caravaggio*," *Storia dell'arte* 9, 10, 1971.

38 "*halls, withdrawing rooms, chambers and antechambers*." F. Borsi, *Palazzo Madama*. Rome, 1960.

39 "*the easy sybaritic existence*." Hibbard, *Caravaggio*.

40 *The earliest known description*. Corradino and Marini, "The Earliest Account of Caravaggio in Rome."

42 *"the last sodomite."* D. Jarman, *Caravaggio* (film script and commentaries). London, 1986.

43 *The cardinal would have regarded them as images of platonic love*. M. Marini, *Michelangelo Merisi da Caravaggio, "pictor praestantissimus."* Rome, 1987.

44 *girlish, Adonis-like looks.* Gilbert, *Caravaggio and His Two Cardinals.*

44 "*his owne boy or servant that laid with him.*" M. Beal, *A Study of Richard Symonds.* London, 1984.

51 *bringing back its luminous quality.* R. Vodret, *"Il restauro del 'Narciso,'"* in *Michelangelo Merisi da Caravaggio* (ed. Macioce), Rome, 1997.

52 *beginning to be recognized all over Rome.* "The Roman World of Caravaggio," in *The Age of Caravaggio* (exhibition catalogue). New York, 1985.

53 *This painting, rediscovered in 1969.* Calvesi, *La realtà del Caravaggio.*

54 *The killing of Count Cenci.* C. Ricci, *Beatrice Cenci.* Rome, 1923.

60 *He shaves the monster's skull.* Ariosto, *Orlando Furioso*, Canto XV.

61 "*it is too natural.*" C. C. Malvasia, *Felsina pittrice. Vite de' pittori bolognesi.* Bologna, 1841.

62 "*Beheading is significant.*" C. G. Jung, *Mysterium Coniunctionis.* London, 1963.

64 *still at San Luigi dei Francesi.* G. A. Dell' Acqua and M. Cinotti, *Il Caravaggio e le sue grandi opere da San Luigi dei Francesi.* Milan, 1971.

65 *King Hyrcanus of Ethiopia.* Jacobus de Voragine, *Legenda Aurea.* Dresden, 1846.

65 *"savage blood-lust."* J. A. Symonds, *The Renaissance in Italy: The Catholic Reaction.* London, 1886.

66 *the Neoplatonist heretic.* F. A. Yates, *Giordano Bruno and the Hermetic Tradition.* London, 1964.

68 *the brothers Cardinal Girolamo Mattei and Marchese Ciriaco Mattei.* Gilbert, *Caravaggio and His Two Cardinals.*

69 *the brothers shared a palace.* S. Danesi Squarzina, *Caravaggio e i Giustiniani,* in *Michelangelo Merisi da Caravaggio* (ed. Macioce).

71 *to signify inspiration.* R. Serracino-Inglott, *Caravaggio: The Symbolism of a Realist*, in *Caravaggio in Malta* (ed. P. Farrrugia Randon). Malta, 1989.

71 *"death as illumination."* P. Askew, *Caravaggio's Death of the Virgin.* Princeton, 1990.

73 *he seems to have read Baronius's* Roman Martyrology. A. Zuccari, *Storia e tradizione nell' iconographia religiosa del Caravaggio,* in *Michelangelo Merisi da Caravaggio* (ed. Macioce).

74 *If he really did paint Baronius.* J. T. Spike, "*Un ritratto del Cardinale Baronio agli Uffizi di Firenza,*" in *La regola*, 1995.

74 *the Cupid's homoerotic quality.* "a boy of the streets and an object of pederastic interest," Hibbard, *Caravaggio.*

76 *the sinister robber gangs*. R. Bassani and F. Bellini, *Caravaggio assassino. La carriera di un 'valenthuomo' fazioso nella Roma della Controriforma*. Rome, 1994.

77 *rooms in the Campo Marzio*. R. Bassani and F. Bellini, "*La casa, le 'robbe,' lo studio del Caravaggio a Roma. Due documenti inediti del 1603 e del 1605*," *Prospettiva* 71 (1993).

78 *a disorderly private life*. Dell' Acqua and Cinotti, *Il Caravaggio e le sui grandi opere da San Luigi dei Francesi.*

80 *A Florentine Knight of Malta*. As a Tuscan, Fra' Ainolfo may have been acting on Grand Duke Ferdinand's instructions. S. Corradini, "*Nuove e false notizie sulla presenza del Caravaggio in Roma*," in *Michelangelo Merisi da Caravaggio,* ed. Macioce.

82 *Passignano's picture was "terrible."* F. Baldinucci, *Notizie dei professori del disegno da Cimabue*, vol 3. Florence, 1847.

83 *a prostitute*. Piazza Navona was where prostitutes plied for hire.

83 "*had had commerce with her*." Hibbard, *Caravaggio.*

83 *brought before the magistrates not less than eleven times*. S. Corradini, *Caravaggio. Materiali per un processo*. Rome, 1993.

85 *a tiny brick building*. The latest research indicates that the masonry is Galilean, even if this does not prove the house arrived supernaturally. N. Monelli, *La Santa Casa a Loreto—La Santa Casa a Nazareth.* Loreto, 1992.

91 *the mild-mannered, gentle-seeming Cardinal Borghese*. L. von Pastor, *History of the Popes*, vol. 25, *Paul V (1605–1621)*. London, 1934.

91 *"a peculiarly rugged disposition."* L. von Ranke, *History of the Popes* (trans. G. R. Dennis), vol 2. London, 1908.

94 *the kind of lighting fashionable in films of the 1920s*. K. Clark, *Civilisation*. London, 1968.

96 *a mixture of rage and fear*. Tasso, *Gerusalemme liberata*, canto XII, stanza 55—"*Non schivar, non parar, non ritirarsi. . . .*"

97 *the reverse was true*. S. Macioce, "*Attorno a Caravaggio. Notizie d' archivio*," *Storia dell'Arte* 55 (1987).

98 *"under guard."* Corradini. *Caravaggio. Materiali per un processo.*

101 *the summer of 1606*. A. Banti (ed.), *Europa mille seicentosei. Diario di viaggio di Bernardo Bizoni*. Rome, 1942.

101 *she had often been in Rome*. Calvesi, *La realtà del Caravaggio*.

102 *"till near sunset."* Augustus Hare, *Days Near Rome*. London, 1875.

103 *Fra' Orazio Giustiniani*. F. Ashford, "Caravaggio's Stay in Malta," *The Burlington Magazine,* June 1935.

106 *he was paid two hundred ducats at Naples*. V. Pacelli, "New Documents Concerning Caravaggio in Naples, *The Burlington Magazine,* December 1977.

106 *Fabrizio Sforza Colonna*. B. Dal Pozzo, *Historia della Sacra Religione Militare di San Giovanni Gerosolomitano*, vol. 2, Verona, 1716.

107 *it seems likely that Caravaggio called on the cardinal.* Z. Wazbinski, "*Il Viaggio del Cardinale Francesco Maria Del Monte a Napoli negli anni 1607–1608,*" in *Michelangelo Merisi da Caravaggio,* ed. Macioce.

108 *Naples the pleasantest of cities.* George Sandys, *A Relation of a Journey begun An. Dom. 1610.* London, 1615.

110 *"received with great acclaim."* M. Gregori, "Caravaggio in Naples," in *Painting in Naples 1606–1705* (ed. C. Whitfield and J. Martineau). London, 1982.

110 *The Seven Works of Mercy.* V. Pacelli, *Le Sette Opere di Misericordia.* Salerno, 1984.

114 *heavenly light.* M. Marini, *Caravaggio, Michelangelo Merisi da Caravaggio "pictor praestantissimus."*

115 *Ludovico Cardi.* The bull for Il Cigoli's admission into the order is in Baldinucci, *Notizie dei Professori*, vol. 9. He was admitted "*in gradu Fratrum Militum obedientiae Magistralis*"—the same grade as Caravaggio.

116 *those who were Genoese.* The nobility of Ottavio Costa's sons was publicly questioned by some Italian knights. E. W. Schermerhorn, *Malta of the Knights.* London, 1929.

122 *The first mention of Caravaggio*. J. Azzopardi, "Caravaggio in Malta: An Unpublished Document," in *The Church of St. John in Valletta 1578–1978* (exhibition catalogue). Malta, 1978.

122 *"the painter."* Calvesi believes the Greek painter was Mario Minniti. Calvesi, *La realtà del Caravaggio.*

123 *a battered if well-preserved old noble*. J. Gash, "The Identity of Caravaggio's 'Knight of Malta,'" *The Burlington Magazine,* January 1997.

127 *Alof de Wignancourt*. Dal Pozzo, *Historia della Sacra Religione*, vol. 2.

128 "*Fra' Ippolito Malaspina*." S. Macioce, "*Caravaggio a Malta e suoi referenti: notizie d'archivio," Storia dell'Arte* 81 (1994).

128 *the Comte de Brie*. Dal Pozzo, *Historia della Sacra Religione*, vol. 2.

130 *a magistral bull*. J. Azzopardi, "Documentary Sources on Caravaggio's Stay in Malta," in *Caravaggio in Malta* (ed. Farrugia Randon).

136 *Preti lost his temper*. B. de Dominici, *Vite dei Pittori, Scultori ed Architetti Napoletani*, vol. 4. Naples, 1846.

140 *"living grave."* D. Calnan, *Knights in Durance*. Malta, 1966.

141 *In front of the oratory's altar*. Stone, "The Context of Caravaggio's 'Beheading of St. John' in Malta." *The Burlington Magazine*, January 1997.

144 *Orecchio di Dionigi*. A. Hare, *Cities of Southern Italy and Sicily*. London, 1883.

145 *Minniti had become a well-established local painter*. F. Campagna Cicala, "*Intorno all' attività di Caravaggio in Sicilia. Due momenti del caravaggismo siciliano. Mario Minniti e Alonso Rodriguez*," *Caravaggismo in Sicilia, il suo tempo, il suo influsso* (exhibition catalogue). Palermo, 1984.

147 *"every chance of seeing the storm lanterns hoisted."* F. Braudel, *La Mediterranée à l'Epoque de Philippe II*. Paris, 1966.

149 *their city's semi-independent status*. D. Mack-Smith, *A History of Sicily*, vol. 1 (800–1713). London, 1968.

153 *the* Madonna della Lettera. T. S. Hughes, *Travels in Sicily, Greece and Albania*. London, 1820.

153 *"down every steep street."* Hare, *Cities of Southern Italy and Sicily*.

154 *schoolmasters had a very unpleasant reputation for pederasty*. Gilbert, *Caravaggio and His Two Cardinals*.

155 *a visitor to the fair*. Lithgow, *The Totall Discourse of the Rare Adventures and painfull Peregrinations of long nineteen Yeares*. London, 1632.

157 *"life was dominated by the Inquisition."* Hibbard, *Caravaggio*.

159 *the Marchesa di Caravaggio's palace on the Riviera di Chiaia*. V. Pacelli, *"La morte di Caravaggio e alcuni suoi dipinti da documenti inediti," Studi di Storia dell'Arte* 2 (1992).

160 *or pouring mercury into their mouths as they slept*. Christopher Marlowe, *Edward the Second*. London, 1594—Lightborn's speech, "I learn'd in Naples how to poison flowers."

161 *a letter to Prince Marcantonio*. F. Bologna and V. Pacelli, "*Caravaggio, 1610: la "Sant' Orsola confitto dal Tiranno" per Marcantonio Doria. 1. Le evidenze documentarie . . .* ," *Prospettiva* 23 (1980).

163 *an* Annunciation. Now in the Musée des Beaux Arts, Nancy. Could this commission have come through the duke of Lorraine's son, the Comte de Brie, who had been his contemporary in the novitiate on Malta?

164 *one foot still inside the grave*. L. Scaramuccia, *Le finezze de' penelli italiani*. Pavia, 1674.

165 *A recently discovered report*. Pacelli, *La morte di Caravaggio*.

166 *a fishing hamlet guarded by a fort*. Hare, *Days Near Rome*.

167 *a document*. M. Marini, "*Caravaggio: l'ultima spiaggia. Port' Ercole . . . un nuovo documento,*" *Il Tempo,* July 18, 1995.

168 *wrapped in a knight's choir mantle*. By custom, even today, the knights are buried in their choir mantles instead of in shrouds.

168 *an official fabrication . . . to conceal his murder*. V. Pacelli, "*Una nuova ipotesi sulla morte di Michelangelo Merisi di Caravaggio,*" in *Michelangelo Merisi da Caravaggio* (ed. Macioce).

169 *a document.* O. H. Green and D. Mahon, "Caravaggio's Death: A New Document," *The Burlington Magazine*, June 1951.

170 *Marino . . . published some affectionate verses.* The poem's full text, taken from Bellori, is in Hibbard, *Caravaggio.*

170 *"such strange behavior."* Haskell, *Patrons and Painters.*

170 *ultimately, he would triumph over sin and death.* S. Rossi, "*Peccato e redenzione negli autoritratti del Caravaggio,*" in *Michelangelo Merisi da Caravaggio* (ed. Macioce).

171 *"Caravaggists."* B. Nicholson, *The International Caravaggesque Movement.* Oxford, 1990.

172 *He was going out of favor.* R. E. Spear, "The Critical Fortunes of a Realist Painter," in *The Age of Caravaggio.*

173 *The* Nativity. F. Watson, *The Caravaggio Conspiracy.* London, 1980.

INDEX

"Academy of those without Senses," 31
Accademia di San Luca, 65
Acquaviva, Claudio, 79, 112
Acripanda (Decio), 40
Adonnino, Count, 152
Adoration of the Shepherds (Caravaggio), 151–152
Adrian VI, Pope, 14
Aldobrandini, Cardinal, 81, 82
Algarotti, Francesco, 172
Amadeus (film), ix
Ameyden, Dirck, 36–37
Aminta (Tasso), 40
Amor Vincit Omnia (Caravaggio), 44, 79
Annunciation (Caravaggio), 163
Antella, Francesco dell', 134
Antico, Catalano l', 152
Antonietti, Amabilia, 83
Antonietti, Maddalena, 83
Arcadelt, Jacob, 43
Aretino (Leonardo Bruni), 35
Ariosto, Ludovico, 59–60
Arpino, Giuseppe Cesari, Cavaliere d', 52, 65, 77, 79–80, 92, 97
  Caravaggio as assistant to, 30–31
  Caravaggio's feud with, 81
  Contarelli Chapel commission and, 63–64
Askew, Pamela, 71

Bacchus (Caravaggio), 43
Bacchus (*Bacchino Malato*) (Caravaggio), 31, 173
Baglione, Giovane, 2, 12, 17, 19, 43, 64, 65, 69, 70, 71, 77, 87, 88, 97, 102, 140, 165, 167, 168, 170, 171
  Caravaggio libel case and, 78–81
  Medusa described by, 60
Barberini, Antonio, 32
Barberini, Maffei, *see* Urban VIII, Pope

Bardi, Fra Ainolfo, 80, 103
Baronius, Cardinal, 25, 69, 73
Caravaggio's portrait of, 74
Baroque Age, 90
Caravaggio's art in context of, 94–95, 171
Counter-Reformation and, 93–94
Baroque art, 15, 50
Basket of Fruit (Caravaggio), 52
Bassani, Riccardo, 76
Beheading of St. John (Campi), 10
Beheading of St. John the Baptist (Caravaggio), viii, 131–134, 141
Beheading of St. John the Baptist (Tibaldi), 10
Bellini, Federico, 76
Bellori, Giovanni Pietro, 2, 9, 11, 12, 17, 19, 29, 40, 47, 48, 51, 65, 69, 71, 72, 77, 87, 92, 93, 97, 99, 102, 103, 116, 134, 140, 144, 147, 151, 154, 156, 157, 160, 161, 165, 167, 169, 171
Beheading of St. John the Baptist described by, 132
Calling of St. Matthew described by, 64
Caravaggio's Malta downfall described by, 135–137
on Caravaggio's use of light-dark contrasts, 52–53
Cardsharps described by, 32
Seven Works of Mercy described by, 111
Berenson, Bernard, ix, 31, 60, 64, 72, 94, 171
Bernini, Gianlorenzo, 50, 67, 91, 92
Bertolotti, Giovanni, 123
Béthune, Philippe de, 80
Bonsanti, Giorgio, 49
Borghese, Camillo, *see* Paul V, Pope
Borghese, Scipione, 99, 101, 129, 130, 137–138, 163, 164, 165
Caravaggio's death and, 168–169
career of, 116–117
described, 92–93
Borromeo, Carlo, 4, 6–7, 10, 17
Caravaggio influenced by, 13–14
Borromeo, Federigo, 31, 35, 52
Bosio, Fra Giacomo, 130
Boy Peeling a Green Citrus Fruit (Caravaggio), 30
Boy with a Basket of Fruit (Caravaggio), 31
Bramante, Donato, 86
Brantôme, Abbé de, 120–121
Braudel, Fernand, 147
Brie, Comte de, 128–129
Brueghel, Jan, 52, 70
Bruni, Prudenzia, 83
Bruno, Giordano, 66–67
Burckhardt, Jacob, 172
Butcher's Shop (Carracci), 47

Caesar, Tiberius, 91
Calling of St. Matthew, The (Caravaggio), 64–66
Bellori's description of, 64
Calvesi, Maurizio, 98
Calvetti, Olympio, 55, 57
Calvi, Domenica, 81–82
Cambiaso, Luca, 70
Camerlengo, Cardinal, 90
Campi, Antonio, 10
Canace (Speroni), 40

Canonico, Flavio, 78
Caproni, Andrea, 56–57
Carafe of Light (Caravaggio), 52
Caravaggio (film), 42
Caravaggio, Lodovico (uncle), 19
Caravaggio, Marchese di, *see* Sforza, Constanza Colonna
Caravaggio, Michelangelo Merisi da:
- attempted murder of, 160–161
- birth of, 2, 12
- death of, 167–168
- described, 40, 77
- education level of, 73
- fame, recognition of, 31, 52, 54, 65, 110, 150
- family background of, 2–4
- friends of, 73, 77–78
- Leoni's portrait of, 174
- personality of, ix-x, 67, 77–78, 152, 170
- religion and, 27–28, 67
- sexuality of, 42–46, 80
- violence of daily life and, 23–24
- in violent episodes, 78–79, 82–84

Caravaggio, Michelangelo Merisi da, art of:
- alchemical symbolism in, 35–36, 62
- apprenticeship in, 9–12
- artificial light and, 53
- in Baroque context, 94–95, 171
- Borromeo's influence on, 13–14
- chiaroscuro in, 10, 49, 52–53, 64, 172
- decapitation theme in, 59–62
- female nudes in, 42
- Giorgione's influence on, 11
- history's assessment of, 171–172
- homosexuality and, 43–45
- lack of fresco training and, 11, 28, 53, 63–64
- last works of, 161, 162
- light as symbol in, 70–71, 94, 112, 114
- models for, 50–51, 61, 71–72, 73, 83, 87, 111, 125, 132, 134
- mystical experience in, 49–50
- naturalism in, 11, 15–16
- nature as subject of, 47
- Oratorians and, 27, 28
- portraits in, 73–74, 93
- religiousness of, 15–16, 27, 28, 48–49, 66–67, 71, 75, 95, 162, 170
- of second Naples period, 161–163
- secular themes in, 67, 170
- self-portraits in, 31, 60, 61, 62, 65, 163, 170
- still lifes in, 51–52
- women in, 42, 45, 125

Caravaggio, Pollidoro da, 3
Caravaggio assassino (Bassani and Bellini), 76
Cardi, Ludovico "Il Cigolo," 82, 89, 116
Cardsharps, The (Caravaggio), 33, 38, 173
- Bellori's description of, 32

Carracci, Annibale, 47, 61, 70, 80
Cassar, Paolo, 122
Catalano (coachman), 55
Catholic Church, 6
- Council of Trent and, 13–15
- Italy ruled by, 25–26

Cavalleti, Ermete, 86–87
Cenci, Beatrice, 55–56, 57, 58, 67

Cenci, Bernardo, 55–56, 58
Cenci, Francesco, 54, 55, 103
Cenci, Giacomo, 55–56, 57, 58, 103
Cenci, Lucrezia, 55–58
Cesari, Tiberio, 70
Cesarini, Duke, 56
Charles I, King of England, 72, 171
Cherubini, Laerzio, 71, 72
Christ at Emmaus (Caravaggio), 103
Christ Carrying the Cross (Caravaggio), 152
Cinotti, Mia, 173
Civilisation (Clark), xvii
Clark, Kenneth, xvii, 94
  Caravaggio described by, 173–174
Clement VIII, Pope, 24, 25, 26, 30, 36, 54, 56, 66, 74, 81, 90, 91, 112
Clement XIV, Pope, 171
Cointrel, Matthieu, 63, 64
Colonna, Ascanio, 102
Colonna, Filippo, 104–105
Colonna, Marcantonio, 4
Colonna, Marzio, 102–103, 111
Combat Between Tancredi and Clorinda (Monteverdi), 96
Concert of Youths (Caravaggio), 38, 47, 50
  homosexuality in, 43–44, 45
Confraternity of Santa Cruz, 168, 169
Considerations on Painting (Mancini), 1–2, 17
Conversion of St. Paul (Caravaggio), 70, 71, 112
Conversion of the Magdalene (Caravaggio), 50–51, 61
Corberio, Eufrosina, 56
Cornacchia (Caravaggio's dog), 82, 144
Coryate, Tom, 3, 4
Costa, Ottavio, 88, 101, 103, 115, 134, 165
Council of Trent, 6, 13–15, 26, 35, 87
Counter-Reformation, 6, 13–16, 26, 37, 48, 90, 95
  Baroque Age and, 93–94
Courtesan "Phyllis," The (Caravaggio), 51, 173
"Cowardize, the Mother of Crueltie" (Montaigne), 96
Crescenzi, Giacomo, 72
Crescenzi family, 74
Crowning with Thorns (Caravaggio), 88
Crucifixion (Carracci), 47–48
Crucifixion of St. Andrew (Caravaggio), 113–114
Crucifixion of St. Peter (Caravaggio), 70
Crucifixion of St. Peter (Passignano), 82
Crucifixion of St. Peter (Reni), 82

dall' Pozzo, Andrea, 128
David and Goliath (Caravaggio), 44
  later versions of, 162–163, 170
Da Vinci, Leonardo, 42
Death of the Virgin (Caravaggio), 71–72, 73, 164
Decio, Filippo, 40
del Monte, Francesco Maria Bourbon, ix, 1, 33, 49, 52, 54, 60, 63, 64, 67, 69, 74, 77, 78, 80, 83, 88, 101, 106, 128
  career of, 34–35
  picture collection of, 38
  sexuality of, 36–37, 42, 44, 46

del Monte, Guidobaldi, 35
Denial of St. Peter (Caravaggio), 162
de Sales, François, 43
Dialogo (Gilio), 14
Divine Love (Baglione), 79
Dolce, Lodovico, 40
Dominicans, 112–113
Dominicis, Bernardo de, 110
Doria, Marcantonio, 88, 161, 162, 165

Ecce Homo (Caravaggio), 88–89
Ecstasy of St. Francis (Caravaggio), 79
Entombment of Christ (Caravaggio), 72–73
Essay on Painting (Algarotti), 172
Este, Cesare d', 87–88
Evelyn, John, 4, 108

Farnese, Alessandro, 37
Farnese, Clelia Facia, 37
Farnese, Odoardo, 47
Flagellation of Christ (Caravaggio), 113
Fortune Teller, The (Caravaggio), 32, 47
  later version of, 39
France, 26, 80, 90
Franchis, Lorenzo dei, 113
Franchis, Tommaso dei, 113
Franco, Cirillo, 14
Frederick II, Holy Roman Emperor, 145
Fry, Roger, 172

Gentile, Deodato, 165, 169
Gentileschi, Orazio, 79
Gerusalemme Liberata (Tasso), 40, 96, 116
Giacomo, Niccolo di, 152
Gilio, Andrea, 14
Giorgione da Castelfranco, 11
Giraldi, Giambattista, 39–40
Giustiniani, Benedetto, 69–70, 74, 79, 101, 103, 165, 169
Giustiniani, Orazio, 103
Giustiniani, Vincenzo, 51–52, 69–70, 71, 72, 74, 88, 99, 101, 103, 116, 165, 169
Golden Legend, The (Voragine), 64–65, 162
  St. Andrew account in, 113
  St. Jerome account in, 92
  St. Lucy account in, 145–146
Gonzaga, Ferdinando, 164, 165
Gonzaga, Vincenzo, 72
Grammatica, Antiveduto, 30
Gregori, Mina, 173
Guercino (Giovanni Barbieri), 67

Hare, Augustus, 102, 103, 153
Henry II, Duke of Lorraine, 163
Henry IV, King of France, 26
Hibbard, Howard, 45, 124
Hoefnagel, Georg, 79
Honthorst, Gerrit van, 70
Humiliati, 7

Incredulity of St. Thomas (Caravaggio), 70
Inquisition, 26, 67, 99, 122, 157–158
Inspiration of St. Matthew, The (Caravaggio), 72, 173
Introduction de la Vie Dévote (de Sales), 43

Italy, ix, 15, 18, 94
Catholic Church rule in, 25–26

James, Henry, 3, 13
Jarman, Derek, 42
Jesuits, 27–28, 153
Dominicans vs., 112–113
Joseph II, King of Germany, 171
Judith and Holofernes (Caravaggio), viii, 60–61, 88, 173
later version of, 111
Judith and Holofernes (Michelangelo), 61
Judith and Holofernes (Minniti), 62
Jung, Carl Gustav, 62

Knights of Malta, *see* Order of Malta

Lanzi, Luigi, 172
Lazzari, Giovanni Battista de, 150
Lena (model), 83, 87, 111
Leo XI, Pope, 91
Leonardo da Vinci, 42
Leoni, Ottavio, 174
Liberati, Francesco, 3, 39
Lithgow, William, 86, 99, 143
Lives of Modern Painters, Sculptors and Architects (Bellori), 9
Lives of the Painters (Baglione), 17
Lomazzo, Giovan Paolo, 10
Lomellini, Fra Francesco, 130
Longhi, Caterina, 74
Longhi, Onorio, 73, 74, 77, 78, 79, 80
Tommasoni affair and, 97, 98–99
Longhi, Roberto, 51, 172
Loreto shrine, 85–87
Lotto, Lorenzo, 86
Louis XIV, King of France, 171
Lute Player, The (Caravaggio), viii, 38–39, 43, 47, 50

Madonna dei Palafrenieri (Caravaggio), 99
Madonna di Loreto (Madonna dei Pellegrini) (Caravaggio), 87, 88, 111
Madonna of the Rosary, The (Caravaggio), 88, 103, 111, 112–113, 171
Mahon, Denis, 161
Malaspina, Fra Ippolito, 103, 104, 115, 123, 128, 134
Malta, 124–126
Caravaggio's escape from, 139–141
see also Order of Malta
Mancini, Giulio, 1–2, 11, 12, 17, 19, 71–72, 97, 102, 103, 167, 168, 171
Mander, Carel van, 76, 85
Mannerism, 15, 47
Marchese, Giacomo, 122, 154
Marianna (Dolce), 40
Marini, Maurizio, 167–168
Marino, Cavaliere, 73, 74, 78, 170
Martelli, Fra Antonio, 123, 154, 173
Martyrdom of St. Matthew, The (Caravaggio), 64–65, 66
Martyrdom of St. Matthew, The (Muziano), 68
Martyrdom of St. Ursula (Caravaggio), 161–162, 164
Mary Magdalene (Caravaggio), 102
Massa, Lanfranco, 161–162
Massimi, Luca, 56
Massimi, Marcantonio, 56

Massimi, Monsignor, 89
Mattei, Ciriaco, 68, 69, 70
Mattei, Giovan Battista, 68
Mattei, Girolamo, 68, 71
Medici, Alessandro de', 91
Medici, Bianca de', 37
Medici, Ferdinando de', 34–35, 37, 54, 74, 80
Medici, Francesco de', 37
Medusa (Caravaggio), 60, 62
Melandroni, Fillide, 50–51, 61
Mengs, Anton Rafael, 172
Menicuccia, 81–82
Merisi, Caterina, 18
Merisi, Fermo di Bernardino, 2–4, 9
  death of, 8
Merisi, Giovan Battista, 1–2, 18
Merisi, Giovan Pietro, 18
Merisi, Giulio, 2
Merisi, Lucia Aratori, 2, 9–10
Messina, 149–150, 158
  Pepe incident in, 154–155
Michelangelo, 14, 42, 47
Microcosmo della Pittura (Scannelli), 162
Milan, Duchy of, 3, 4–5
  Caravaggio's flight from, 18–19
  plague epidemic in, 7–8
  violent crime in, 17–18
Minniti, Mario, 30, 34, 43, 44, 45, 62, 76, 77–78, 98, 145, 147
Mirabella, Vincenzo, 144–145
models:
  for Caravaggio, 50–51, 61, 71–72, 73, 83, 87, 111, 125, 132, 134
  as prostitutes, 50–51, 61, 71–72, 83, 132
Montaigne, Michel de, 18, 25, 40–41, 45–46, 50, 56, 96
  Rome experiences of, 20, 21, 22–23
Monteverdi, Claudio, 96
Montoya, Pedro, 43
Moryson, Fynes, 104, 107, 109
Mozart, Wolfgang Amadeus, ix
Muziano, Girolamo, 68
Mysterium Coniunctionis (Jung), 62

Naples:
  altarpieces for, 110–114
  Caravaggio's first sojourn in, 106–108
  Caravaggio's second sojourn in, 159–160
Narcissus (Caravaggio), 51, 73
Nashe, Thomas, 21, 39, 109
Nativity (Caravaggio), 157, 173
Nativity with St. Francis and St. Lawrence (Caravaggio), 173
Neoplatonists, 31, 36, 67
Neri, Filippo, 69, 73, 74

Oratorians, 27, 28
Orbeche (Giraldi), 39–40
Order of Malta, 10, 84, 135, 144, 154, 168
  Caravaggio as novice in, 122–123
  Caravaggio ejected from, 141–142
  Caravaggio's ambition to enter, 103–104, 115–117
  Caravaggio takes vows in, 133–134
  daily life of, 124–125
  history of, 119–120
  importance of St. John to, 131–132
  Wignancourt as grand master of, 127–129

Orlando Furioso (Ariosto), 59–60
Orsi, Aurelio, 73, 98
Orsi, Prospero, 32
Orsola, Sister, 162
Our Lord at the Breaking of Bread, see Supper at Emmaus, The

Paladino, Filippo, 152
Paleotti, Gabriele, 35
Palermo, 156–157
Palestrina, Giovanni, 14
Papal States, 25
Pasqualone, Mariano, 82–83, 88, 161
Passignano (Domenico Cresti), 82
Pastor Friso (Caravaggio), 68
Paul V, Pope, 90, 91–92, 95, 106, 112, 130, 164, 170
  Caravaggio's portrait of, 93
Penitent Magdalene (Caravaggio), 48
Penitent Magdalen (lost) (Caravaggio), 42
Pepe, Carlo, 154–155
Peretti family, 30
Perfetto Maestro di Case, Il (Perfect Master of the Household) (Liberati), 3, 39
Peterzano, Simone, 10–11
Petronio (Antonio da Bologna), 97, 98
Philip II, King of Spain, 5, 6–7, 131
Pius IV, Pope, 6
plague, 7
Poussin, Nicolas, 171
Preti, Fra Mattia, 116, 136
prostitutes, models as, 50–51, 61, 71–72, 81–82, 83, 132
Protestantism, 14, 15
Pucci, Pandolfo, 29–30

Radolovich, Nicholas, 110
Raising of Lazarus, The (Caravaggio), 150–152, 154
Ranke, Leopold von, 91
Raphael, 21, 65
Relatione della citta di Roma (Ameyden), 36
Reni, Guido, 82
Rest on the Flight into Egypt (Caravaggio), viii, 48–49
Resurrection (Baglione), 79
Resurrection of Christ (Caravaggio), 164
Roman Martyrology (Baronius), 73
Rome:
  Caravaggio's flight from, 99-102
  Cenci murder scandal in, 54, 55–56
  daily life in, 20–22
  disastrous floods in, 54–55
  papal domination of, 25–27
  violence in, 22–24
Roncalli, Cristofero, 80
Rubens, Peter Paul, 67, 72
Ruskin, John, 172

Sacrifice of Abraham, The (Caravaggio), 73
St. Catherine of Alexandria (Caravaggio), 50, 61
St. Francis in Ecstasy (Caravaggio), 49–50
St. Francis Receiving the Stigmata (Caravaggio), 164
St. Jerome (Caravaggio), 115, 123, 173
St. John the Baptist (Caravaggio), 88–9
  see also Pastor Friso

St. John the Baptist in the Wilderness (Caravaggio), 169
St. Matthew and the Angel (Caravaggio), 72
Salini, Mao (Tommaso), 80
Sandrart, Joachim von, 74, 77, 81, 84, 97, 116, 123–124, 169–170
Sandys, George, 108, 124, 125, 127, 132, 145, 147, 149
Sangallo, Antonio da, 86
Sansovino, Jacopo, 35
Santa Croce, Paolo di, 57
Scannelli, Francesco, 162
Schubert, Franz, 46
Seven Works of Mercy, The (Caravaggio), 110–111
sexuality:
  of Caravaggio, 42–46, 80
  of del Monte, 36–37, 42, 44, 46
  Renaissance conceptions of, 42–43
Sforza, Alessandro, 34
Sforza, Fra Constanza Colonna, 2, 4, 30, 103, 106, 117, 169, 173
  Caravaggio aided by, 99, 101–102, 159, 160–161
Sforza, Francesco, 2, 3, 4
Sforza-Colonna, Fra Fabrizio, 106, 118, 119
Siciliano, Lorenzo, 30
Sicily, 143, 149
Sixtus V, Pope, 21, 24, 30, 35, 83
  reign of, 25–26
Sleeping Cupid (Caravaggio), 134
Spain, 5, 26, 90, 107, 108
Spata, Costantino, 40
Speroni, Sperone, 40
Spiritual Exercises (Jesuits), 28
Stampa, Girolamo, 78
Supper at Emmaus, The (Caravaggio), viii, 68–69
  second version of, 103
Susannah and the Elders (Caravaggio), 42
Susinno, Francesco, 117, 135–136, 140, 143–144, 146, 147, 154, 156, 157
  Caravaggio's Messina sojourn described by, 150–153
Symonds, John Addington, 65, 172
Symonds, Richard, 44

Taking of Christ (Caravaggio), 69, 71, 173
Tasso, Torquato, 40, 74, 96, 116
Taverna, Ferrante, 80
Tempesta, Antonio, 80
Theatines, 27
Tibaldi, Pellegrino, 10
Titian, 3, 10, 35
Tommasoni, Alessandro, 98
Tommasoni, Giovan Francesco, 97, 98
Tommasoni, Ranuccio, 96–98, 104, 109, 111, 117, 135, 137, 142, 173
Tooth-Drawer, The (Caravaggio), 162
Tullio, Marco, 78

Urban VIII, Pope (Maffei Barberini), 36, 37, 73–74
Urbino, Duke of, 35, 169

Valentin, Maître, 32, 33
violence:
  Caravaggio and, 23–24, 78–79, 82–84
  in Milan, 17–18
  in Rome, 22–24

Vittrici family, 72–73
Voragine, Jacobus de, 64–65

Wignancourt, Fra Alof de, 115–116, 117, 121, 123, 126, 138, 140, 141, 161
  background of, 127
  as grand master of Order of Malta, 127–129

Youth Bitten by a Green Lizard (Caravaggio), 30

Zerafa, Marius, 173
Zola, Emile, 172
Zuccari, Federico, 80
Zúñiga y Requeséns, Luís de, 5